The Sierra Gateway Map Guide

"Where to Stay,
What to Do,
Things to See"

By Debora and Ed Delaney

Published by Talahi Media Arts
Prather, California

The Publisher: Talahi Media Arts
26178 Whispering Oak Lane
P.O. Box 360
Prather, CA 93651
USA

Website: http://www.Talahi.com

The information in *"The Sierra Gateway Map Guide"* is presented to help travelers experience not only the traditional vacation spots, but also the lesser known, but equally beautiful off the beaten path places in the Sierra Nevada. Like the Interactive SierraGatewayMap.com on which this book is based, it includes a wealth of web sites to allow you to see, in greater detail, exactly what there is to see and do in the expansive area it covers.

The Sierra Gateway Map Guide provides many safety tips concerning driving, weather, wildlife and traveling in general. Always use sound judgment and good decision making to insure your trip is pleasurable and safe.

ISBN: 0-9706798-0-7
Printed by The Banta Books Group, Spanish Forks, Utah

Contents

Preface

California's towering Sierra Nevada are among the most beautiful mountains in the world. Whatever the season, Mother Nature treats you to breathtaking scenes, using them as a backdrop. Dipping her brush into a palette containing every color of the rainbow, her artistic strokes highlight the streams, trees, stars, lakes, flowers, sky, abundant wildlife, clouds, chiseled granite and everything else in her domain.

The *Sierra Gateway Map Guide* provides great insight into many fantastic "off the beaten path" destinations. Many travelers, foreign and domestic, yearn to see the back roads. Naturally, the well known locations - Yosemite, Sequoia and Kings Canyon National Parks - are well documented herein. But what lies around and in between them? Step into the *Sierra Gateway Map Guide* and see for yourself.

The authors have based this *Guide* on their popular interactive Internet web creation, the SierraGatewayMap.com. Using this web based tool, anyone, anywhere in the world, can get a wonderful insight into the incredible beauty that awaits them, in and around the Sierra Nevada. In the comfort of their home, families can review destinations, determine what activities are offered, see accommodations that are available and contact local businesses, directly via email or by clicking on one of the hundreds of linked merchant web sites.

This *Guide* is your travel companion as its presents scores of detailed maps, hundreds of full-color photographs and excellent up-to-date information on what to see, where to stay and things to do, year around. Find a Kiosk with a computer and Email a merchant, ask a question, make a reservation. It is designed to fit into your purse, backpack, glove box or pocket as you travel. It will help you figure how to get from here to there and everywhere in between!

Meanwhile, if you have a question, at home, or on the road, email the authors at info@SierraGatewayMap.com.

Introduction

The *Sierra Gateway Map Guide* thoroughly takes you into one of the premier vacation regions in the world! It covers the "usual" spots and takes you a step further, depicting a multitude of lesser known destinations.

Running nearly 400 miles, from just south of Lassen Peak to Tehachapi Pass, the Sierra Nevada is a major mountain range. It's tallest point, Mt. Whitney, rises 14,494 feet above sea level, and is the tallest peak in the contiguous U. S. Coincidentally, the lowest point on the continent, Death Valley, at 282 feet below sea level, is but a short drive from Mt. Whitney.

From a geological standpoint, this range is a single block of the earth's crust, tilted upward toward the east. The slopes are covered with great forests. Miners found large quantities of gold embedded in quartz, while silver finds flourished on the eastern slopes. It's home to national forests and parks. The Pacific Crest National Trail winds it way through the rugged range and is a popular trek for visitors from around the world.

The Sierra Nevada's dramatic eastern escarpment rises sharply above the Great Basin deserts. The region is important to California, as a source of numerous rivers and for its scenic beauty. No other area in the country approaches the plant variety found here. Nearly 40 percent of plant species found naturally in the U.S. are indigenous to California, many of them in these mountains, known for spring-blooming wildflowers, with the California poppy and lupine being the most common.

A Great Basin bristlecone pine, said to be over 4,000 years old, is considered the world's oldest living tree. It stands in the eastern Sierra Nevada. Giant sequoias are found here as well, many over 2,000 years old. Quiet, lush meadows are common in the Sierra Nevada above the timberline.

The abundant vegetation provides a natural habitat for many different animals. You'll see coyotes, rabbits, foxes, squirrels, beaver, bobcats, cougars, deer, skunk, raccoons, elk, pronghorn antelope, bear, mountain goats, marmots and rattlesnakes. A variety of birds also populate the Sierra Nevada. The most notable are eagles, ducks, geese, owls, woodpeckers, jays, crows, osprey, road runners, hummingbirds, finches and sparrows. Countless lakes, streams and rivers are home to trout, including golden, rainbow, German brown and brook. You'll also find pike, catfish and salmon.

Therefore, no matter what outdoor events excite you, this is the place to go. Year round activities are almost too numerous to mention, but here goes anyway: Fishing, camping, golfing, river rafting, hiking, rock climbing, alpine skiing, mountain biking, hunting, rock collecting, sightseeing, cross country skiing, horseback riding, snow boarding, boating, swimming, water skiing, photography, sailing, jet skiing, snowmobile trail riding or just enjoying a good book! There are numerous historical sites and museums to check out too!

Use this *Guide to* better understand and navigate California's Sierra Nevada during your visit. There are more than 80 detailed area maps to help you get from here to there. There are over 300 full-color photographs depicting just what you might expect to see and experience during your travels.

Detailed information is provided on three national parks: Kings County, Sequoia and Yosemite; five national forests: Inyo, Sequoia, Sierra, Stanislaus and Toiyabe; eight wilderness areas: Ansel Adams, Carson-Iceberg, Dinkey Lakes, Domeland, Emigrant, Golden Trout, Hoover, Jennie Lakes, John Muir, Kaiser, Mokelumne, Monarch and South Sierra; and nine counties in and around the Sierra Nevada: Calaveras, Fresno, Inyo, Kern, Madera, Mariposa, Mono, Tulare and Tuolumne.

Phone numbers, addresses, web sites and email listings are provided for your convenience. Find a Kiosk, local library or other facility with a computer during your trip, get on-line and request any data you need from Sierra Nevada businesses.

Herein you'll find nearly everything you'll need to make your vacation successful. No matter if you're from around the corner or the other side of the world, this *Guide* will provide you with valuable information. Jump right in and enjoy yourself!

Ansel Adams Wilderness

Formerly the Minarets, this area was renamed in 1984 to honor the famous photographer and environmentalist.

It covers over 220,000 acres, including the rugged high country east of the Sierra crest, plus the North, Middle and lower South Forks of the San Joaquin River. It offers spectacular alpine scenery and deep granite-walled gorges.

Yosemite National Park borders the Wilderness on one side, while the John Muir Wilderness borders it on the other side.

Elevations range from 7,000 to nearly 14,000 feet with the lower levels having small plateaus, perennial streams and numerous lakes. The area is popular with backpackers from around the world.

Pack trains of horses and mules are very common.

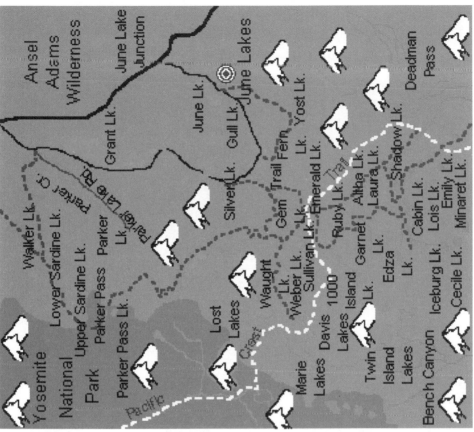

Abundant wildlife, good fishing, coupled with beautiful scenery makes this a great spot to visit. To reduce impact on plant and animal life, overnight trailhead quotas are in effect from July 1 through Labor Day for most trails. You'll want to get a wilderness permit, which is required to enter the back country in most areas. These permits play an important part in protecting the land from overuse, while providing a more enjoyable experience for the traveler and also act as a safety precaution for the user.

Keep in mind that bikes and any motorized vehicles are prohibited in all wilderness areas. Pets and firearms are permitted in National Park wilderness areas.

There are four main points used to enter the Ansel Adams Wilderness. Each has complete information on the specific trails you may want to travel. The 1964 Wilderness Act established a program intended to preserve unique wild and scenic areas of America's public lands.

It defined wilderness as "an area where the earth and its community of life are untrammeled by man, where man himself is a visitor who does not remain." Each of us can help by observing **NO TRACE** camping practices and leaving the areas we visit as undisturbed as possible. Be very careful with campfires, food storage and water used for drinking. Days are generally sunny with cool to cold nights. Summer storms can sneak up on you!

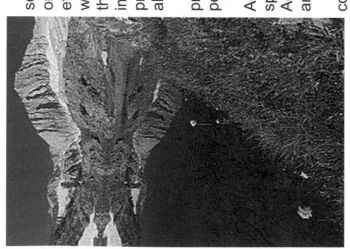

Spectacular views are found throughout the Ansel Adams Wilderness

2

West Side Entry
South of San Joaquin River
Pineridge Ranger District
(559) 841-3311

West Side Entry
North of San Joaquin River
Meadow
Minarets Ranger District

East Side Entry
June Lake Loop to Tioga pass
Mono Lake Ranger District
(760) 647-6525

East Side Entry
Reds Meadow to Agnew

Mammoth Ranger District

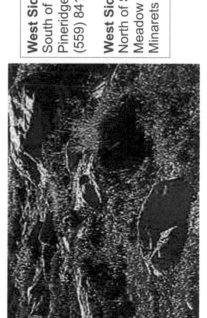

3

Calaveras County

*Home
of the
Celebrated
Jumping Frog!*

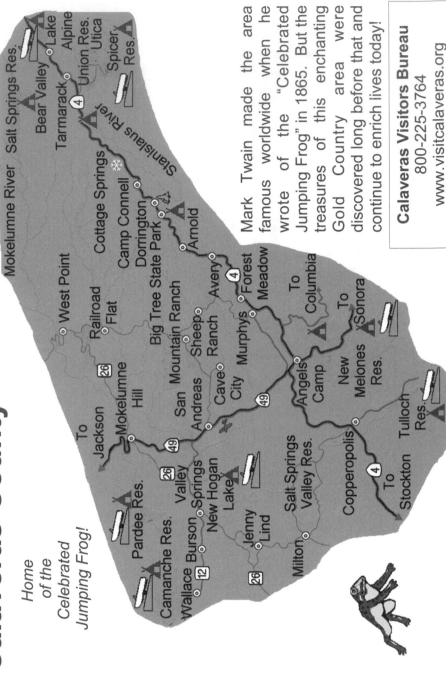

Mark Twain made the area famous worldwide when he wrote of the "Celebrated Jumping Frog" in 1865. But the treasures of this enchanting Gold Country area were discovered long before that and continue to enrich lives today!

Calaveras Visitors Bureau
800-225-3764
www.visitcalaveras.org

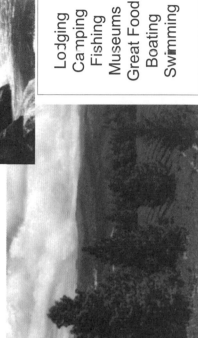

Located in the foothills, 133 miles east of San Francisco and 135 miles west of Lake Tahoe, Calaveras County is filled with natural and historic diversity. Pan for gold, visit historic museums, play golf, explore caverns, browse through countless antique shops.

Travel the hiking and biking trails. Camp, fish, ski, go horseback riding or enjoy a houseboat outing. Take a snowmobile ride or spend some time ice skating.

Make plans to join the fun at the Calaveras County Fair and Jumping Frog Jubilee, always the last weekend in May. It's a great outing for all the family.

Lodging
Camping
Fishing
Museums
Great Food
Boating
Swimming

Named after Henry Angel, who traveled from Rhode Island and opened a trading post here in 1848, Angels Camp is the only incorporated city in all of Calaveras County! It was a teeming mining town and is honey combed with tunnels from the many successful mines. Spend a day with a "Walking Tour & Driving Map".

With it you can enjoy the day visiting many interesting points of this lively old community. You'll want to spend some time at the Angels Camp Museum. It is filled with lovingly preserved artifacts from the Gold Rush era and features several fascinating outdoor exhibits, including a blacksmith's shop, a unique carriage house and a collection of mining equipment.

There's plenty of good "eats", comfortable lodging, and things to do. Tour the caverns, play golf, enjoy a beautiful lake with fishing and houseboat rentals or just wander through the many historic buildings and monuments.

Mark Twain once lived in a cabin, not far from town. In 1864, he wrote his first successful short story "The Celebrated Jumping Frog of Calaveras County". The community celebrates the book's theme annually, with a family-fun filled old time County Fair!

Angels Camp Business Assn.
www.angelscamp.com
Museum
(209) 736-2963

Come Up to Arnolds!

During the Gold Rush era, this area was home to two large ranches involved in logging. Bob and Bernice Arnold arrived in 1927 and built the Ebbetts Pass Inn. Nature surrounds the town, which sits snugly in the Stanislaus National Forest. Naturally there's all the traditional outdoor activities to enjoy, along with the Sierra Nevada Logging Museum!

Camping
Fishing
Swimming
Biking
Boating/Rafting
Camping
Skiing
Horseback
Riding
Hiking
Backpacking
Golf/Tennis

**Greater Arnold
Business Association**
(800) 225-3764
(209) 795-0904

Bear Valley Mountain Resort

Whether you enjoy racing downhill or trucking along a groomed cross country trail, this is the place to be. Year round resort features family snow sports and spectacular summer adventures.

Consider joining the festivities that surround the Annual Aire Bear and Ski Fest. Contact the resort for full details!

Open year round. Picnic areas, 120 campsites and Visitor's Center

Calaveras Big Trees State Park

Few places in the world can match the natural beauty, about four miles above Arnold on Highway 4, where you'll find Giant Sequoias. These trees range in size from 325 feet high, to 24 feet in diameter. Some are said to be 2,000 years old.

The fossil remains of the massive trees indicate they lived with the dinosaurs and other prehistoric creatures that roamed the earth millions of years ago. At the South Grove, there's a self guided tour four-mile trail that winds through a virtually untouched grove of these giant trees.

Visitor's Center - (209) 795-3840
Park Office - (209) 795-2334

9

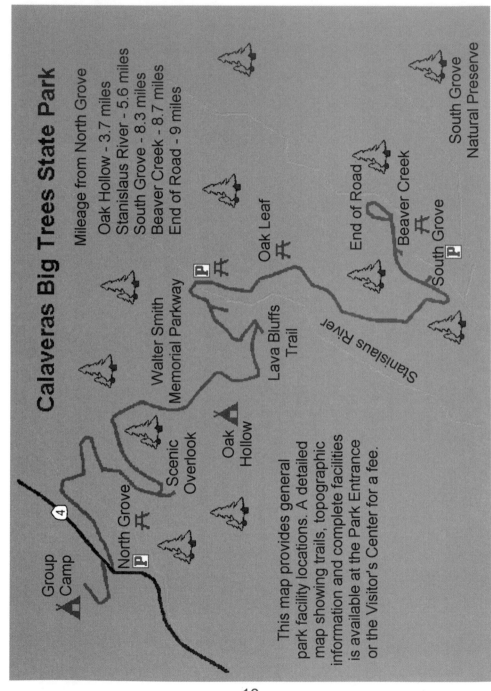

Calaveras Big Trees State Park

Mileage from North Grove

Oak Hollow - 3.7 miles
Stanislaus River - 5.6 miles
South Grove - 8.3 miles
Beaver Creek - 8.7 miles
End of Road - 9 miles

Group Camp

North Grove

Scenic Overlook

Oak Hollow

Walter Smith Memorial Parkway

Oak Leaf

Lava Bluffs Trail

Stanislaus River

End of Road

Beaver Creek

South Grove

South Grove Natural Preserve

This map provides general park facility locations. A detailed map showing trails, topographic information and complete facilities is available at the Park Entrance or the Visitor's Center for a fee.

Copperopolis

The history of Copperopolis is closely tied to the Civil War, and the notorious outlaw Black Bart. The 19 million pounds of copper mined in the 1860's made Calaveras County second in national production of this ore.

The bandit, born Charles E. Boles, came to the California gold fields in 1852, after abandoning his wife and children in Illinois. Using the name Bolton, he worked the area as a miner, which didn't work well for him, because he soon took up robbing Wells Fargo stagecoaches. His first and last holdups took place near Copperopolis. Dressed in a white linen duster, cloth-wrapped boots and sporting a flour sack with eye holes cut in it, he talked his way into his first strong box. After his third robbery, he left a poem staing his dislike of Wells Fargo. It was signed Black Bart, the "Po8". His final robbery was marked by the first time shots were fired at him. He was hit and left a laundry marked kerchief at the scene, which led lawmen to his identity. He was caught, confessed to the last stickup and was convicted in the San Andreas Courthouse. Though questioned, he was never tried for any other robberies attributed to Black Bart! He served six years at San Quentin, was released and vanished without a trace. In all, he took nearly $18,000 from Wells Fargo.

You can see some mining and workshop sites, plus historical artifacts from this era that remain alongside buildings that have been restored. It is also close to popular Lake Tulloch and a great golf course.

Mokelumne Hill

Today you're more likely to hear a coyote howling than an ole miner. But 150 years ago, the miners definitely made more noise than these four-legged evening musicians.

Found in 1848, Moke Hill, as it was known then, was amongst the richest mining spots in California. It was the county seat in the early days, and even for the times, the town was quite a violent place to be.

As the gold played out, Mokelumne Hill shrunk from a wild and woolly 15,000 to the much less populated, quiet historic village that it is today. The main street is directly adjacent to Highway 49 between San Andreas and Jackson. It's well worth the stop. Many of the original buidlings still stand. Wander over to the historic Hotel Leger. You're liable to hear some real tall tales about cattle stampedes in the middle of the night or stories about heart wrenching sobs of a jilted lover that still come from one of the hotel's rooms. All the work of ghosts. Really!!!!

You can also visit the nearby French Hill Winery and the California Caverns at Cave City about eight miles from San Andreas. Production is very limited and only premium quality wines are bottled. The tasting room has art, jewelry and other gift items. French Hill is open weekends from 11 am to 5 pm.

Since 1850, California Caverns attracted visitors with it's large rooms, miles of winding passages, deep black lakes and unique formations. It takes over an hour to cover the lighted trails. You can take a special trip, with professional guides , deep into the earth, across underground lakes and into areas not on the regular tour.

California Caverns
(209) 736-2708
www.caverntours.com
French Hill Winery
(209) 286-1800
www.Frenchhill.com
Mokelumne Hill Historical Society
(209) 286-1770

Murphys Historic Hotel & Lodge once the Sperry & Perry Hotel

Sometimes called the Queen of the Sierra, this quaint old town is now known for its many natural attractions, like the caverns, an old and charming Main Street, a setting of friendly store owners and their very unique shops.

Nearby are some of California's lesser known, yet very excellent wineries awaiting your visit. Each is within a four mile radius of the town square. You can actually tour many of them riding in style in an old time carriage.

You can round out the day playing golf, or try to see how good you are at gold panning. You'll find excellent lodging, tasty meals, and a very delightful destination to bring the entire family.

Big Trees Carriage Company
(209) 728-2602
Black Sheep Winery
(209) 728-2157
www.blacksheepwinery.com
Chatom Vineyard
(209) 736-6500
www.chatomvineyards.com
Ironstone Vineyards
(209) 728-1251
www.ironstonevineyards.com
Mercer Caverns
(209) 728-2101
www.mercercaverns.com
Milliaire Winery
(209) 728-1658
www.milliairewinery.com
Stevenot Winery
(209) 728-3436
www.stevenotwinery.com

The Stanislaus River - Enjoy the beauty, see the power!

Lots of potential for enjoyable outdoor experience: hiking, boating, photography, picnicking, fishing, wildlife viewing and camping are but a few examples. All parks offer picnicking facilities, restrooms and access to the river. Historic buildings and access to the upper river canyon draw visitors to the Knights Ferry Recreation Area, but visitors to the lower parks will enjoy the quiet river landscape. Come and explore!

Hiking trails in Goodwin Canyon, Knights Ferry, Orange Blossom, Valley Oak and McHenry Avenue offer short tours of lush river woodlands. The four miles of rapids above Knights Ferry draw white-water enthusiasts from throughout the world.

Bring your own or rent equipment from one of several local concessionaires. The use of motorized boats is limited. It's always a good idea to check the river flow before boating. The river is open to fishing from January 1 to March 31, and the 4th Saturday in May to October 15 each year.

Trout, small-mouth bass, striped bass, carp, channel and white catfish and black crappie tempt anglers. The entire river is closed to fishing from October 16 - December 31 for protection of the fall Chinook salmon run.

Stanislaus River Parks Headquarters
(209) 881-3517
stanislaus-info@spk.usace.army.mil
OARS Outdoor Adventure River Specialists
(209) 736-4677
www.oars.com
Beyond Limits Adventures
(800) 234-7238 or (209) 869-606
www.rivertrip.com

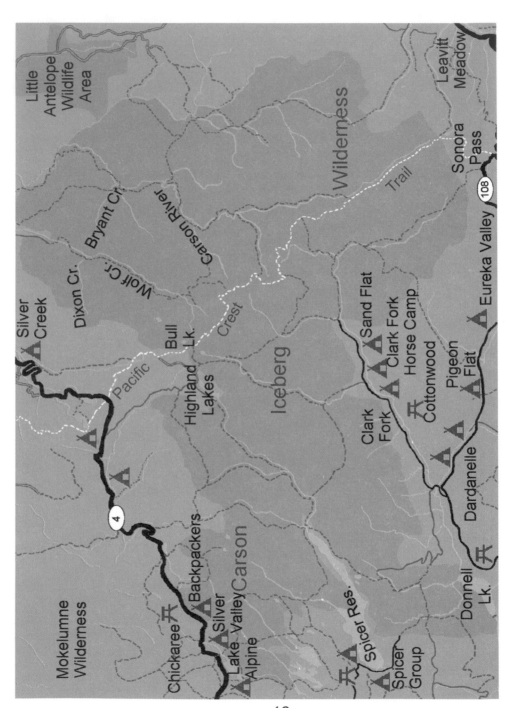

The 160,000 acre Carson-Iceberg Wilderness straddles central Sierra Nevada crest in the Stanislaus and Toiyabe National Forests. It lies within Tuolumne and Alpine Counties and is only bordered by Highway 108 on the south and Highway 4 on the north. Watersheds drain to the Stanislaus and Carson Rivers.

The name Carson-Iceberg comes from the Carson River and the "The Iceberg", a distinctive granite formation near Clark Fork Road. Carson-Iceberg is a rugged landscape of great scenic beauty, dominated by volcanic ridges and peaks. Prominent in the southwest are the Dardanelles. Many streams flow through deep granite canyons, but there are few lakes. Elevations range from 5000 feet near Donnell Reservoir to 11,462 feet at Sonora Peak.

One can see a vast desert to the east and a dense conifer forest to the west. Snow can linger into June, later following very wet winters. Summers are generally dry and mild, with periodic afternoon thundershowers and very cold nighttime temperatures. People who use the Carson-Icebeg Wilderness visit primarily from June through September. Most use is concentrated around the few lakes found here. By applying no-trace camping skills, visitors can minimize the impact of recreational use on the wilderness environment.

Information about "leave no trace" skills can be found on wilderness permit attachments and is posted at trail heads. Please help by keeping gates closed. For 10,000 years, various Native Americans inhabited the area, most recently, the Me Wuk from the west slope and the Washoe of the Great Basin.

They spent the warmer months hunting in the high country and trading with each other. In 1827, Jedediah Smith and fellow trappers crossed from the east somewhere near Ebbetts Pass. The earliest emigrant crossing was in 1841 by the Bartleson-Bidwell party, just north of Sonora Pass. Following the discovery of gold in 1848, native cultures quickly declined. Sheep and cattle grazing became the major use of this area. Grazing continues to this day, but recreation has now become the dominant use. There are approximately 195 miles of trails in the Wilderness. Travel is restricted to foot or horseback.

Major trailheads on the Stanislaus portion are Wheat's Meadow, County Line, Arnot Creek, Disaster Creek, and Clark Fork on the Summit Ranger District (Highway 108) and Silver Valley (Lake Alpine), Stanislaus Meadow, Mosquito Lakes, Pacific Valley, and Highland Lakes on the Calaveras Ranger District (Highway 4). A Wilderness Visitor's Permit is required for overnight visits. Permits and Wilderness maps can be purchased at any National Forest office.

Death Valley National Park

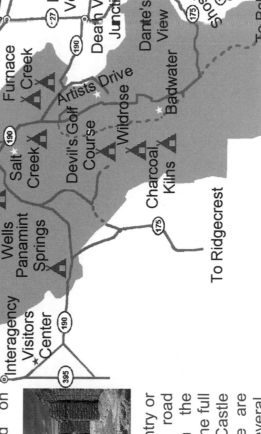

To Big Pine

To Tonopah

Scotty's Castle ★

Ubehebe Crater ★

Grapevine

Rhyolite ★

Mesquite Springs ▲

Titus Canyon

Sand Dunes ★

Stovepipe Wells ▲

Panamint Springs ▲

Lone Pine

Interagency Visitors Center ★

Beatty

Furnace Creek ▲

Salt Creek ▲

Devil's Golf Course

Artists Drive

Wildrose ★

Charcoal Kilns ▲

Badwater ★

Dante's View

Death Valley Junction

To Las Vegas

Lathrop Wells

Shoshone

To Baker

To Ridgecrest

In Death Valley's three million acres, there are 350 miles of roads, many unpaved. Vehicles with high-clearance are suggested, four-wheel-drive is better. Bikes are allowed on

roads, but not for cross-country or on hiking trails. The basic road tour of scenic sights in the Furnace Creek area takes one full day. The tour of Scotty's Castle requires a half day. There are many campgrounds open, several

19

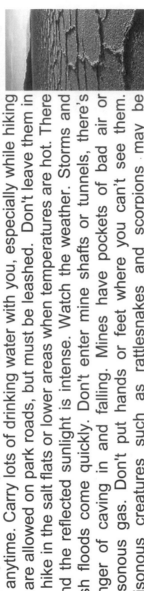

in the back country. Death Valley summers are extremely hot, winters are mild with occasional storms. Use sun protection, wear sturdy walking shoes, sunglasses and a broad-rimmed hat. In winter you need warmer clothes and a jacket. Dehydration is dangerous, and can hit you anytime. Carry lots of drinking water with you, especially while hiking or biking. Pets are allowed on park roads, but must be leashed. Don't leave them in vehicles. Don't hike in the salt flats or lower areas when temperatures are hot. There is no shade and the reflected sunlight is intense. Watch the weather. Storms and flash floods come quickly. Don't enter mine shafts or tunnels, there's danger of caving in and falling. Mines have pockets of bad air or poisonous gas. Don't put hands or feet where you can't see them. Poisonous creatures such as rattlesnakes and scorpions may be sheltered there. Watch your vehicle's temperature. Turn off the A/C on uphill grades. If the engine overheats, allow the motor to idle rather than turning it off. Slowly pour water over the radiator to cool it. Add water to the overflow container if needed. Stay with your car if it breaks down.

Your car will provide shade. Others will come by before you can walk for help. You'll need to fill out a voluntary Back Country Camping Permit, if you are planning an overnight hike. Furnace Creek Visitor Center has a museum, information desk and book store. Stovepipe Wells Village has a fee station and Scotty's Castle features a

bookstore and museum.

Dinkey Lakes Wilderness

This area includes many miles of scenic hiking and OHV trails which meander along trout laden streams, over dramatic granite outcropping and through beautiful lush meadows.

The forest ranges from moderate to heavily forested. Elevations range from 8,000 feet to 10,619 feet at Three Sisters Peak.

There are many easy to access small lakes, yielding lots of hard fighting trout. A wide variety of wildlife await you. If you enjoy bird watching, you'll return to relieve the experience. It's a favorite location for family picnics, day hikers as well as backpackers and horseback riders.

Spring and summer days are usually sunny, with a chance of a thunderstorm always present. The evenings are cool and overnight it can get real cold.

You can reach the wilderness area via Kaiser Pass Road (north), Red/Coyote Jeep Road (west), Rock Creek Road (southwest) or Courtright Reservoir (southeast). It is accessable from mid-June to late October. There is no quota system in effect at this time, but you will need a Visitor Permit for all overnight stays.

These permits play an important part in protecting the land from overuse, while providing a more enjoyable experience for the traveler and also act as a safety precaution for the user. You may obtain

one from the local ranger station.

There's an excellent family oriented campground at Dinkey Creek, beyond the store and ranger station. Just up the hill from the camp sites is a great spot for swimming.

Several easy to challenging trails lead from the general area. Thirteen lakes are a short distance away. One trail takes you to an old logging town with some interesting structures still standing.

22

The McKinley Grove of giant sequoias is not far from the Dinkey Creek campground. It has a shaded picnic area and an easy trail that takes you through the big trees.

Kids enjoy fishing the creek by the bridge that leads towards Wishon and Courtright Reservoirs. It is stocked weekly during fishing season. Be careful, it can run very swiftly during the late spring, and the rocks are slippery.

If you are interested in a horseback riding experience, a pack station is near. They offer hourly rides and also can assist you in planning a trip into the back country. One such trip features the studying of the flora and fauna found in the Sierra Nevada.

Whether you're staying in the campground or going on into the backcountry, it's important that you be aware of bears. You must use the containers that are provided in the campground or take a canister with you on overnight hikes. Otherwise, use food caching techniques that allow you to hang the food from a tree, out of a bear's reach.

It's easy to get here. Just take Highway 168 from the Clovis-Fresno area. You can also come up along the King's River above Pine Flat Lake. Most of it is a rough, narrow road. However, it is very scenic. You can see the Black Rock Lake campground and Upper King's River.

23

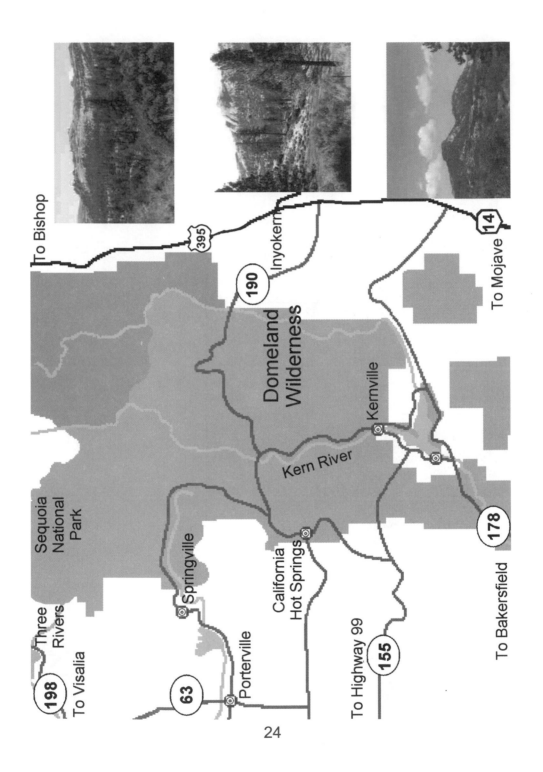

To Bishop

395

Inyokern

190

14

To Mojave

Domeland Wilderness

Kernville

Kern River

Sequoia National Park

Three Rivers

198

To Visalia

Springville

Porterville

63

California Hot Springs

To Highway 99

155

178

To Bakersfield

Domeland Wilderness

In addition to a hat and something to help block the mid-day sun, it's a good idea to bring along a comfortable pair of hiking boots. Or bring a friendly four-footed pack or riding animal, because you won't be using your vehicle around here.

This is definitely hiking and horseback riding country. There are many scenic trails to choose as you explore the Domeland Wilderness. For instance, the Mountain Botanical Area, a 440-acre site on the northern tip of the area, features over 100 species of plants. Some that have been found among the sedimentary rocks have been dated back more than 135 million years. This is surprising and quite unusual in an area that is nearly dominated by granite formations. The biggest plant attraction in the Domeland Wilderness is one known as the Bald Mountain potentilla (Horkelia tularensis). It's famous. It just doesn't occur anywhere else in the world. Plan to work your way to the 40-foot-high fire lookout on the mountain. The trek is more than worthwhile. The view you'll experience is simply spectacular. It spans a breathtaking several hundred square miles of both Domeland and its little neighbor, South Sierra Wilderness Area. In the late spring through early fall, the temperatures during the day can be very high. It is important that you make sure to bring a lot of water to help restore the fluids you will naturally be losing.

Additionally, this is the time of the year to watch out for poisonous rattlesnakes. The Wild and Scenic South Fork of the Kern River crosses the area through deep gorges with bold rock outcroppings and domes interspersed with meadows.

The river and its tributaries attract trout anglers. Fly fishermen will find this an excellent place to tempt a wily trout from the waters.

The Pacific Crest Trail crosses the area north-south and follows the river for about nine miles. Other trails, suitable for foot and horse, give access mostly to the northern section, leaving the south and east seldom explored and difficult to travel.

Sequoia forest visitors are more likely to start their explorations of this upper Kern River Canyon area in Cannell Meadow, which borders the wilderness on the east. The Cannell Meadow and surrounding areas provide a few campgrounds and several pastures for those who bring their own horses.

Campers, hikers, fishing enthusiasts, and backpackers need to know about plants in this part of the forest that cause skin irritation. Try to avoid stinging nettle (Urtica dioica) and poison oak. You also need to be aware of rattlesnakes from April through October. Be very careful if you move rocks or stick your hand anywhere near a hole in the ground.

Rafting on the river is great fun. If you have your own equipment, fantastic. For those who would like to take a professionally guided whitewater rafting trip down the Kern River, there are several outfitters to assist you.

Chuck Richards Whitewater
(760) 379-4444
Kern River Tours
(760) 379-4616
Whitewater Voyages
(800) 400-RAFT
www.whitewatervoyages.com
Sequoia Outdoor Center
(760) 376-3776.
Cannell Meadow Ranger District
(760) 376-3781
Greenhorn Ranger District
(760) 379-5646

Emigrant Wilderness Area

Many 1850's gold seekers made their way to the ore rich California minefields through this particular section of the beautiful Sierra Nevada . Hopefully, they didn't find themselves in the area once the snow began to fall! Travel into Emigrant Wilderness is closed during the winter. Use Highway 108 from Sonora or the Bridgeport area to reach this vacation paradise.

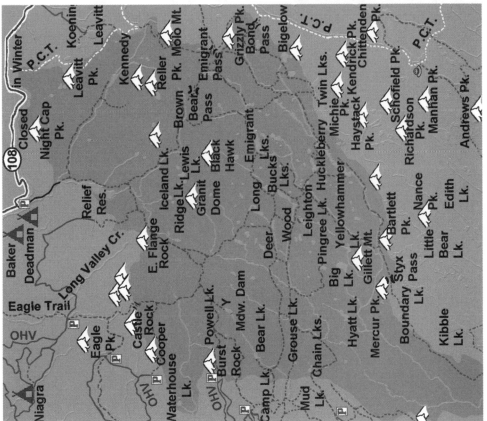

The spectacular 113,000 acre Emigrant Wilderness area is bordered by the world famous Yosemite National Park on the south, the Toiyabe National Forest on the east and Highway 108 on the north. It is a strangely elongated area stretching north-east about 25 miles in length and up to 15 miles in width. The numerous watersheds drain to the Stanislaus and Tuolumne Rivers. This Emigrant Wilderness is entirely within Tuolumne County and is nearly 140 air miles east of San

Francisco and 50 air miles south of Lake Tahoe. The Emigrant Wilderness is blessed with a glaciated landscape of incredible scenic beauty. The northeastern third of the Wilderness is dominated by volcanic ridges and peaks; the remaining areas consist of many sparsely vegetated, granitic ridges interspersed with numerous lakes and lush meadows. Elevations range from below 5000 feet and lush meadows. Elevations range from below 5000 feet near Cherry Reservoir to 11,570 feet at Leavitt Peak, but the

elevation range of most of the popular high use areas is 7500 to 9000 feet. Snowpacks typically linger into June, sometimes later following very wet winters.

Summers are generally dry and mild, with cool evenings and nighttime temperatures can dip below freezing anytime. Afternoon thundershowers occur periodically and can be very intense.

This beautiful Sierra Nevada gem is an outstanding backdrop for fishing, hiking, backpacking, horseback riding and back county pack trips. Photographic possibilities abound!

Permits are required for overnight stays and group size is limited. Travel is restricted to foot or horseback. Mechanized transportation of any kind, including bicycles, is prohibited.

Several trailheads are available. They include Bell Meadow, Crabtree Camp, Gianelli Cabin, and Kennedy Meadows.

Aspen Meadows Pack Station
 (209) 965-3402
Camping Reservations
 (877) 444-6777
 www.reserveusa.com
Dandanelle Resort
 (209) 965-4355
Kennedy Meadows Resort
 (209) 965-3900
 (209) 532-9663
 www.kennedymeadows.com
Sardella's Pack Station
 (209) 965-3402
 (209) 984-5727
Summit Ranger Station
 (209) 965-3434

Fresno County

More Fun Than You Ever Imagined!

From the flatlands of the fertile soiled San Joaquin Valley to the very crest of the Sierra Nevada, this huge geographical area offers the outdoorsman a rich and varied group of activities.

See underground gardens, relax in natural hot springs, enjoy the solitude of wind swept 9,000 foot peaks and marvel at the Giant Sequoias. Test your fly fishing skills, unfurl your sails on a world class High Sierra lake or ride the white water of the mighty King's River. Be sure to bring along your camera and your family!

Fresno County Visitors Guide
www.fresno-county.com

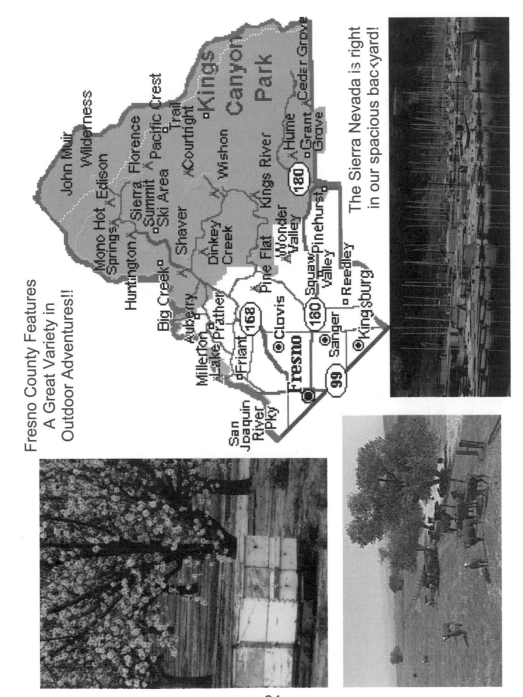

Fresno County Features
A Great Variety in
Outdoor Adventures!!

The Sierra Nevada is right
in our spacious backyard!

John Muir
Wilderness

Mono Hot
Springs
Edison

Florence

Sierra
Summit
Ski Area

Pacific Crest
Trail

Courtright

Kings
Canyon
Park

Wishon

Kings River

Hume

Grant
Grove

Cedar Grove

180

Huntington

Shaver

Dinkey
Creek

Pine Flat

Wonder
Valley

Squaw
Valley

Pinehurst

Reedley

Kingsburg

180

Sanger

Big Creek

Auberry

Prather

Millerton
Lake

Friant

168

Clovis

Fresno

99

San
Joaquin
River
Pky

31

Auberry

Nestled in the foothills, 30 miles east of Fresno, this rural community has a rich history, including ranching, logging and Indian culture. Take a ride up to Squaw Leap and find out how it got that name. Visit the Mono Wind Casino and try your luck. Grab your fishing pole, hike down to the San Joaquin River and rustle up a trout for dinner.

In the spring, you'll wonder at all the scenic beauty of the colorful wildflowers. Drive on down to Jose Basin and wander the back roads up to Big Creek or visit Reddinger Lake. In either case, pack a lunch. There are great places for an afternoon picnic. Bring along your camera!

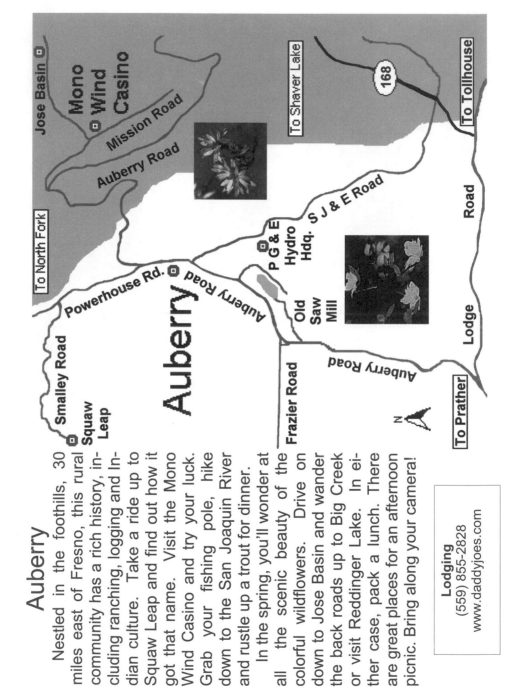

Lodging
(559) 855-2828
www.daddyjoes.com

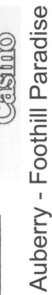

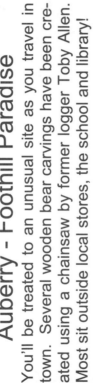

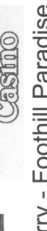

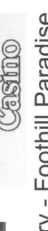

Auberry - Foothill Paradise

You'll be treated to an unusual site as you travel in town. Several wooden bear carvings have been created using a chainsaw by former logger Toby Allen. Most sit outside local stores, the school and library!

33

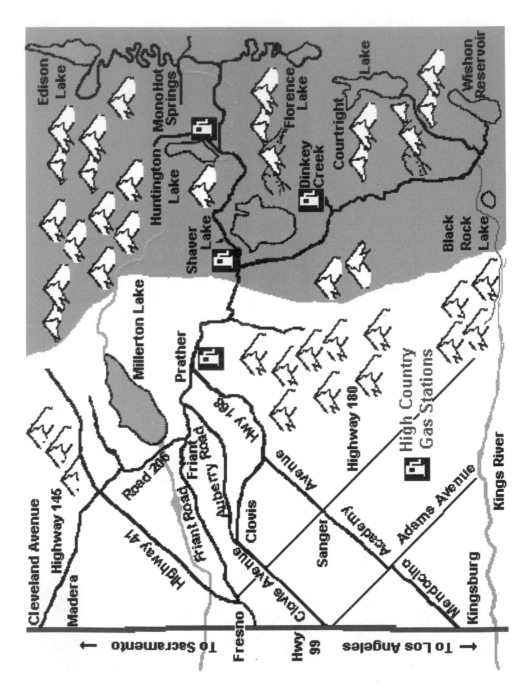

CLOVIS

Known locally as "The Gateway to the Sierras", this community is ready to make your vacation more enjoyable. Annual events include Big Hat Days and the Clovis Rodeo. There's a weekly Friday evening farmer's market in Old Town during the summer months. Complete Services are available.

Clovis Chamber
(559) 299-7363
www.clovischamber.com
Clovis Visitor's Center
(559) 297-2696
(877) 725-6947

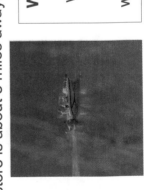

The map shows the Courtright Reservoir area with the following labeled features: Burnt Corral Mdw., Post Corral Cr., Trail, Long Mdw., Corral Mt., North Fork Kings River, Burnt Corral Cr., Chamberlains Camp Station, Maxson Dome, Hobbler Lk., Voyager Rock, Anderson Cr., Long Top, Lost Pk., Dusty Cr., Maxson Mdw., Helms Cr., Dusty Ershum OHV., Courtright Res., Maxson Rock, Marmont Rock, Tunnel Rd., Courtright, Hot Spring Pass, Cliff Lake, Trapper Springs, Wee Mee Kute, Short Hair Mdw.

Courtright Reservoir

Excellent fishing from the shore or a boat is one of the reasons Courtright is such a popular spot for the many visitors that return each year to this high country reservoir. It is one of many that PG&E has built over the years to help generate hydroelectric power. It is fairly isolated. It is usually open from late May through October, depending upon snow conditions. There are nice campgrounds, plus a boat ramp with a dock. Many off-road trails are in the vicinity too. A pack station is near and you can enjoy a trail ride or a backcountry trip. A general store is about 8 miles away. Look out for woodchucks!

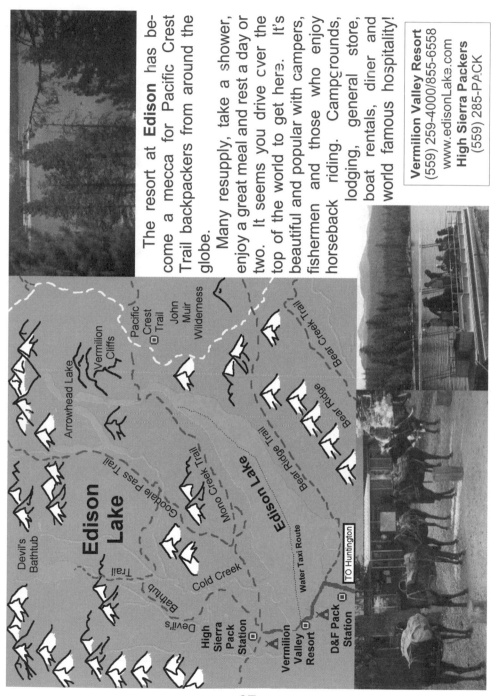

The resort at **Edison** has become a mecca for Pacific Crest Trail backpackers from around the globe.

Many resupply, take a shower, enjoy a great meal and rest a day or two. It seems you drive over the top of the world to get here. It's beautiful and popular with campers, fishermen and those who enjoy horseback riding. Campgrounds, lodging, general store, boat rentals, diner and world famous hospitality!

37

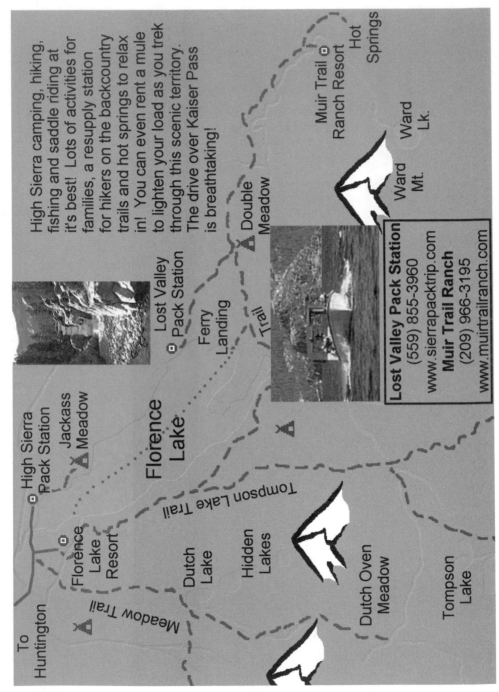

High Sierra camping, hiking, fishing and saddle riding at it's best! Lots of activities for families, a resupply station for hikers on the backcountry trails and hot springs to relax in! You can even rent a mule to lighten your load as you trek through this scenic territory. The drive over Kaiser Pass is breathtaking!

To Huntington

Meadow Trail

Florence Lake Resort

High Sierra Pack Station

Jackass Meadow

Florence Lake

Tompson Lake Trail

Dutch Lake

Hidden Lakes

Dutch Oven Meadow

Tompson Lake

Lost Valley Pack Station

Ferry Landing

Trail

Double Meadow

Muir Trail Ranch Resort

Hot Springs

Ward Mt.

Ward Lk.

Lost Valley Pack Station
(559) 855-3960
www.sierrapacktrip.com
Muir Trail Ranch
(209) 966-3195
www.muirtrailranch.com

38

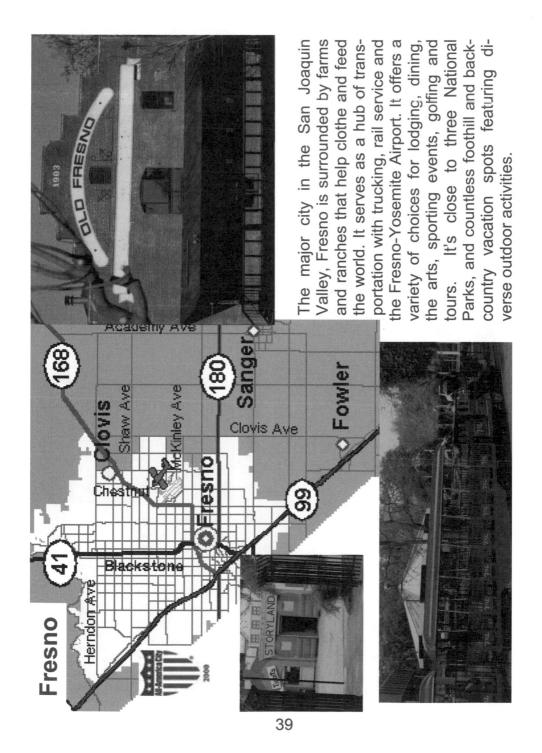

Fresno

The major city in the San Joaquin Valley, Fresno is surrounded by farms and ranches that help clothe and feed the world. It serves as a hub of transportation with trucking, rail service and the Fresno-Yosemite Airport. It offers a variety of choices for lodging, dining, the arts, sporting events, golfing and tours. It's close to three National Parks, and countless foothill and back-country vacation spots featuring diverse outdoor activities.

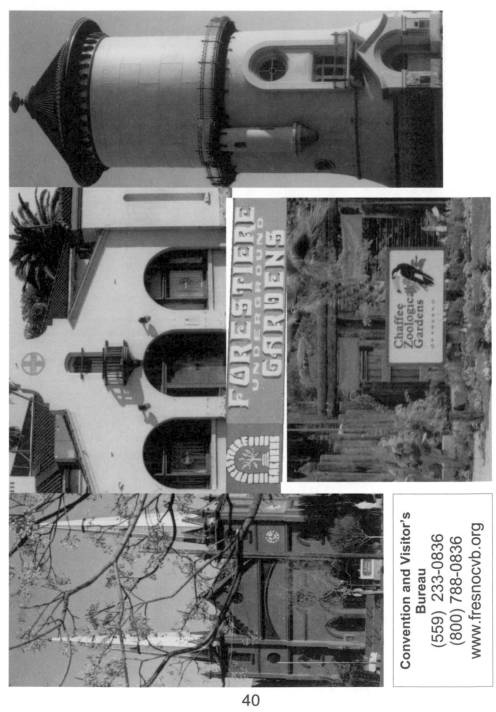

Forestiere Underground Gardens

Chaffee Zoological Gardens OF FRESNO

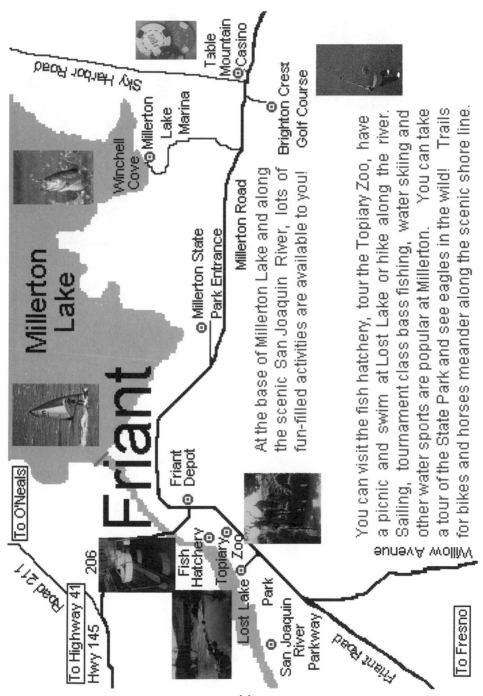

Above, a view of Friant Dam
Below, the Topiary Zoo

Have a picnic at Lost Lake

Take a canoe ride on the river.

At left, are views
of fish hatchery
facilities to tour.

For More
Information
Contact
Friant Depot
(559) 822-4600

Camping and RV Park facilities, general store, Post Office and laundry. Wonderful family setting for fishing, boating, hiking and relaxing. Open June to September. Road closed during the winter months.

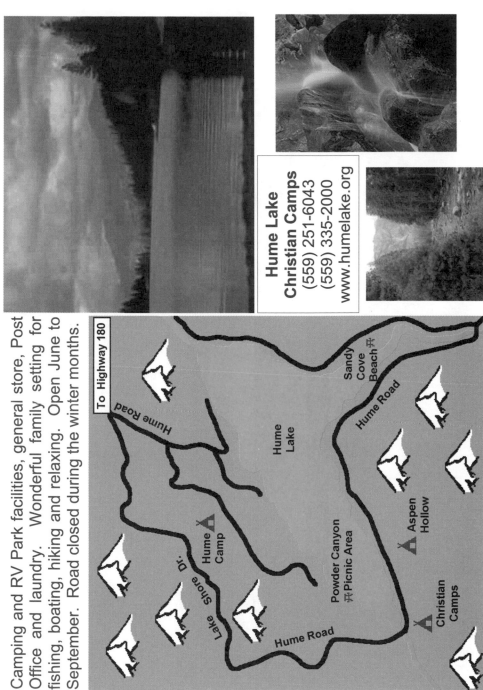

Hume Lake
Christian Camps
(559) 251-6043
(559) 335-2000
www.humelake.org

To Highway 180

Hume Road

Hume Road

Lake Shore Dr.

Hume Camp

Hume Lake

Powder Canyon
Picnic Area

Hume Road

Sandy Cove Beach

Hume Road

Aspen Hollow

Christian Camps

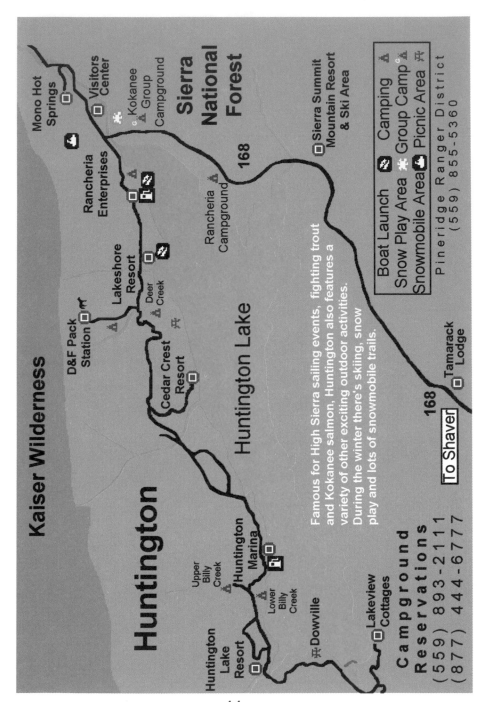

Kaiser Wilderness

Huntington

Mono Hot Springs

Visitors Center

Kokanee Group Campground

Sierra National Forest

168

Sierra Summit Mountain Resort & Ski Area

Rancheria Enterprises

Lakeshore Resort

D&F Pack Station

Deer Creek

Rancheria Campground

Huntington Lake

Cedar Crest Resort

Upper Billy Creek

Huntington Marina

Lower Billy Creek

Dowville

Lakeview Cottages

Huntington Lake Resort

Boat Launch   Camping
Snow Play Area   Group Camp
Snowmobile Area   Picnic Area

Pineridge Ranger District
(559) 855-5360

Famous for High Sierra sailing events, fighting trout and Kokanee salmon, Huntington also features a variety of other exciting outdoor activities. During the winter there's skiing, snow play and lots of snowmobile trails.

168

To Shaver

Tamarack Lodge

Campground Reservations
(559) 893-2111
(877) 444-6777

44

Year around family fun activities, plus great facilities, help make Huntington Lake the Great Place It Is!

45

Cedar Crest Resort

Hidden among the beautiful pines, this facility offers nice lake front cabins, tent cabins, RV spaces with water and electrical hookups, a general store, dining facilities and boat rentals.

It is known for great hospitality, delicious food and its family oriented environment. It is generally opened around May 20 with a normal season running through September.

(559) 893-3233
Winter phone
(619) 442-8616

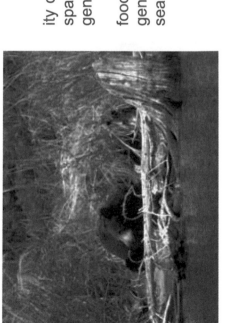

46

D & F Pack Station

Brad Myers has been serving vacationers to the Sierra for over 20 years. Enjoy a leisurely ride in the Huntington area, or have him plan a special backcountry trip for you and your family. Whether it's a ride to fish, hunt, sightsee or "just get away from it all", you'll be pleased you stopped by! Bring your camera, the views are great!

www.highsierrapackers.com
Summer (559) 893-3220
Winter (559) 299-4451

47

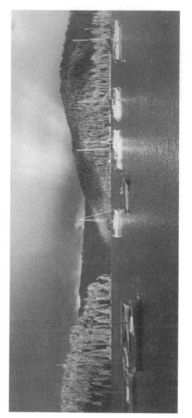

Huntington Lake Marina
(559) 893-6750

If you don't have a watercraft, you can spend the day on the lake with a rented catamaran, fishing boat, jet ski or power boat. There's boat fuel, repair facilities and tackle shop. The restaurant offers up some great meals, while the gift shop surely has a unique treasure for yourself or that someone special! There are many scenic campsites nearby, plus a number of clean, comfortable cabins at reasonable rates.

Huntington Lake Resort

Here at 7,000 feet there's fresh, clean air and plenty to do. Enjoy your stay in a completely outfitted cabin. Wake to the sounds of birds chirping. The spring and summer seasons offer hiking, fishing, sailing, boating, swimming, horseback riding, wind surfing and more. In the winter, there's alpine and cross country skiing and lots of snowmobile trails to ride.

(559) 893-3226

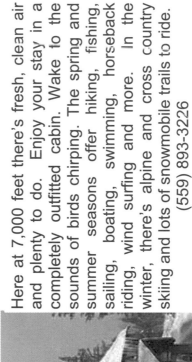

Winter and Summer Activities

Lakeshore Resort

Lakeshore is a unique, rustic old resort. Built in 1922, it features an old time saloon, a full service restaurant, well stocked general store, huge lodge hall, 26 original cabins and a renovated 20 space RV park. It is close to all lakeside activities: swimming, fishing, sailing, water skiing and sun bathing. Boat rentals, fuel and repair service are available.

Just up the road is a complete stable for horseback riding or backcountry trips. Hiking and backpacking trails lead you to fabulous vistas that rival Yosemite. Close by are three wilderness areas: Kaiser, Ansel Adams, and John Muir. Sierra Summit Ski area is 2.5 miles and over 150 miles of snowmobile trails are out the front door. You can venture out on cross country treks right from your cabin! For year round family fun, this is a great place to come and spend a few days.

(559) 893-3193
www.lakeshoreresort.com

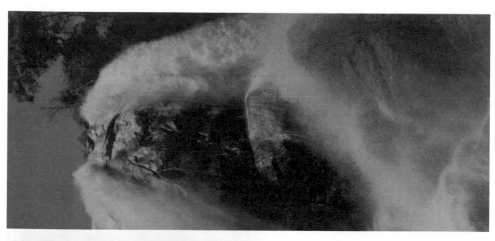

Lakeview Cottages

If you like quiet solitude, these cabins, on the far side of the lake should do just fine. Boat rentals are available too! Hiking trails lead to many high country scenic wonders. Waterfalls and rushing streams afford great picture opportunities. You can picnic nearby at Dowville or drive up and over Kaiser Pass to Mono Hot Springs to experience hot mineral waters. There's always things to see and do. You won't want to leave!

(559) 893-2330
(562) 697-6556

Mono Hot Springs

Mono Hot Springs is located on the South Fork of the San Joaquin River. Here you find a very serene and peaceful atmosphere for the adventurous who really do appreciate truly uncrowded, spectacular scenery deep in the high country of the Sierra Nevada. You'll find family cabins, hot baths, a cafe and general store.

Enjoy healthful hot mineral springs, superb trout fishing, horseback riding, scenic hiking, fantastic photo opportunities, relaxing in the spa, or sun bathing down at the swimming hole.

(559) 325-1710
www.monohotsprings.com

52

Rancheria Enterprises

The friendly Rancheria folks offer a mini-mart, large marina and tackle shop, full service garage, fuel, snowmobile rentals and some fantastic advice.

(559) 893-3234
www.rancheriaenterprises.com

53

SIERRA SUMMIT

Come Up for Some Fantastic Skiing! No matter if your pleasure is alpine or snowboards, whether you're a beginner or former pro, you'll get great enjoyment from the facilities available. The entire staff is trained to ensure your visit is memorable. From ticket sales to equipment rentals, to ski school instructors to lift operators, to the trail grooming crew to food service specialists and the ski patrol members, the Sierra Summit team strives to make your experience one you'll want to repeat, again and again! Lodging, restaurant and RV parking are available to you. Check with the office for special events!

Business Office - Lodging - Events
(559) 893-3311 - (559) 233-1200 - (559) 233-3330
www.sierrasummit.com

54

Tamarack Lodge

Nestled in the pines near Tamarack Creek, a few hundred yards off Highway 168, Tamarack Lodge provides guests with warm, inviting accommodations at surprisingly affordable rates.

Most rooms feature a real woodburning fireplace (with plenty of firewood), knotty pine decor, and kitchen with refrigerator, stove and cooking utensils.

Use Tamarack Lodge as a base to enjoy the outdoor opportunities available to you here in the beautiful Sierra Nevada. Just minutes away is crystal-clear Huntington Lake, for spring and summer activities. In the winter, you're just a short drive from Sierra Summit Ski Resort, offering alpine and snowboard terrain for every level!

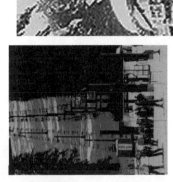

(559) 893-3244

55

Kings Canyon Lodge

Located 17 miles east of Grant Grove, this is a privately owned facility. It features cabins, gasoline and a restaurant. Nearby Boyden Cave is a very interesting cavern to tour.

You'll experience spectacular views of Kings Canyon and the Kings River as you drive on toward Cedar Grove. There you can enjoy fishing, hiking, horseback riding, camping and other out-door adventures.

(559) 335-2405

Valkommen to Kingsburg

Kingsburg is a rural agricultural community in the San Joaquin Valley, regionally famous for its Swedish heritage. The architecture of the town attempts to capture the flavor of a Swedish village. It has a number of excellent places to stay and eat! Plan to attend the big Swedish Festival which is held annually on the third weekend of May. This colorful attraction features great food, costumes and lots of fun! You can choose to secure local lodging and take interesting day trips to the surrounding area. In an hour and half drive you can visit many scenic attractions like the Shaver and Huntington Lake areas, or see the giant trees in Kings Canyon or Sequoia National Parks.

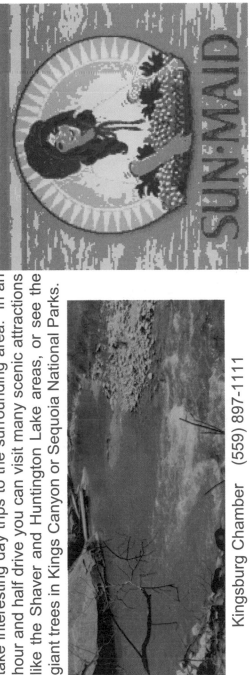

Kingsburg Chamber   (559) 897-1111

57

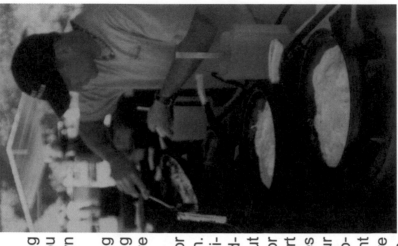

Kings River

Meandering through deep granite lined canyons, carrying Sierra Nevada melting snow, the Kings can mesmerize you as it rushes towards it's destination. Naturally, it's well known for providing the means for exciting white water adventures.

However, the rafting season only spans a few stimulating weeks. It's then you notice the fly fishing enthusiasts moving along the shore, finding pools that may be hiding an elusive rainbow trout.

If you've never tried either of these great outdoor activities, then it's time to plan a visit and do them both. Meanwhile, many trails along the river that head into the Sierra Nevada are popular with those that favor horseback riding. For those without their own river raft or kayak, there are expert river rafting companies that will help make your experience very memorable. You can just rent equipment, or picture this full service adventure. Imagine sleeping under the stars with the sounds of the river close by. You awake to an all you can eat breakfast feast and then board a bus to the river and the awaiting rafts! Bring your wet suit and camera!

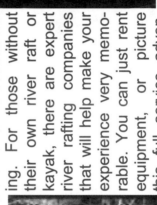

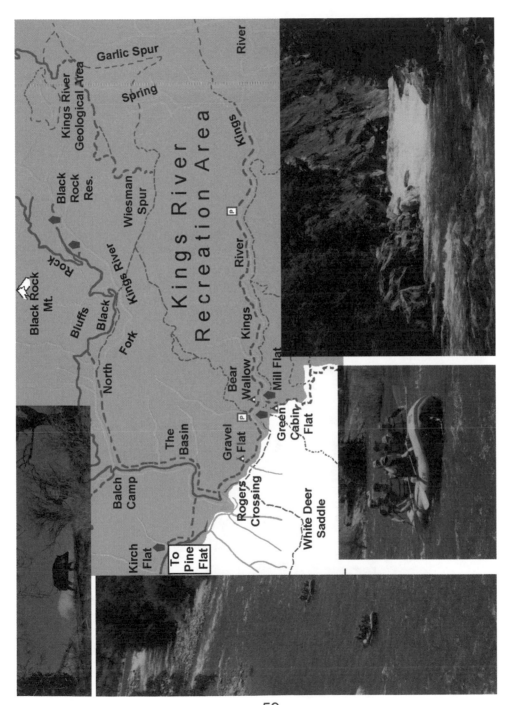

Kings River
Recreation Area

Garlic Spur

Spring

Kings River
Geological Area

River

Kings

Black
Rock
Res.

Wiesman
Spur

Black Rock Mt.

Rock

Bluffs

Kings River

Black

River

Kings

North

Fork

Kings

The Basin

Bear
Wallow

Mill Flat

Gravel
Flat

Green
Cabin
Flat

Balch
Camp

Rogers
Crossing

White Deer
Saddle

Kirch
Flat

To
Pine
Flat

59

While in the area, you should plan to see three very unique characteristics: a wild trout fishery in the Kings River, Garlic Falls and the Boole Tree, recognized as the largest Sequoia found in any National forest in the U.S. It is 289 feet tall and 29 feet in diameter.

Four developed campgrounds and four designated group camping areas are along the Kings. They are free, and available on a first-come, first served basis. A permit is required for the group camping areas. It can be obtained from the Trimmer Ranger Station.

Lodging is available in nearby places like Reedley, Sanger, Wonder Valley and Kingsburg. Supplies can be purchased in the Pine Flats Lake area. This area can be very hot in the summer, so it is more pleasurable to visit in the spring and fall. Watch for out poison oak!

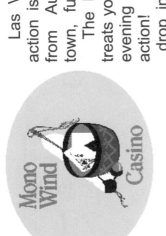

Las Vegas style gaming action is just minutes away from Auberry, the foothill town, full of friendly folks. The Mono Wind Casino treats you to an afternoon or evening of Las Vegas style action! Actually, you can drop in anytime, it's open round the clock. Enjoy a great meal or your favorite beverage while trying your luck. There are special events, holiday celebrations and a variety of entertainment events!

"The Friendliest Little Casino"
(559) 855-4350

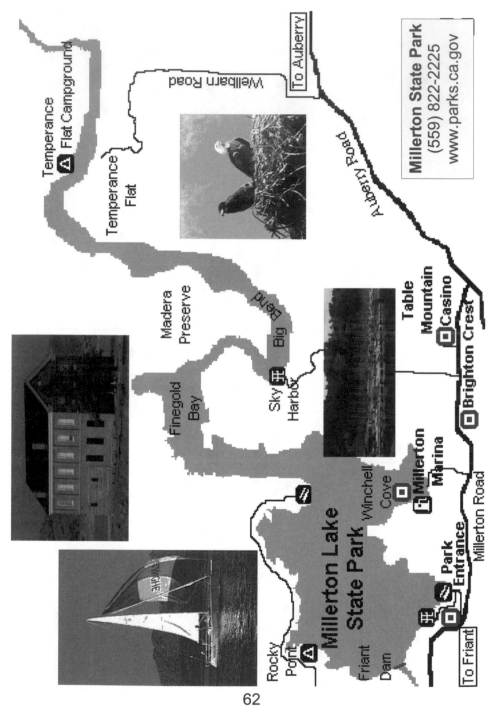

Temperance
Flat Campground

Temperance
Flat

Wellbarn Road

To Auberry

Auberry Road

Millerton State Park
(559) 822-2225
www.parks.ca.gov

Madera
Preserve

Big Sand

Table
Mountain
Casino

Brighton Crest

Finegold
Bay

Sky
Harbor

Millerton
Marina

Millerton Lake
State Park

Winchell
Cove

Park
Entrance

Millerton Road

Rocky
Point

Friant
Dam

To Friant

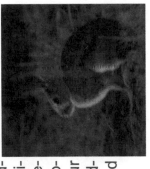

Millerton Lake was created in 1944, when Friant Dam was built across the San Joaquin River. It now boasts over 40 miles of shoreline. As the water filled the terrain behind the new dam, the old Millerton City site was covered. The original Millerton County Courthouse, built in 1867, has been reconstructed. You can tour the distinctive structure. Some say they've seen ghosts move about the historical site. It is located near the dam parking lot.

Camping facilities are numerous and include some primitive sites for boat campers in the Temperance Flat. The sites at the lake feature a Dump Station, Picnic Areas, Showers and Nature Trails. The park is open year round. Summers can be hot, with cool evenings. Spring and fall are mild and the winters tend to be cold. Plan to dress accordingly. The recreational area is a favorite of bass fishermen, water skiers, sailors and swimmers. The marina in Winchell Cove offers gas, repairs, snacks and mooring facilities. The hills surrounding the lake provide excellent treks for hikers and horseback riders. In the winter, tour to see bald and golden eagles that nest locally. You can see other wildlife such as squirrels, cottontail rabbits, mule deer, badgers, coyotes and an occasional cougar.

Millerton State Park Camp Grounds
(559) 822-2225
www.parks.ca.gov

Restrooms
Picnic Area
Campground
Dump Station

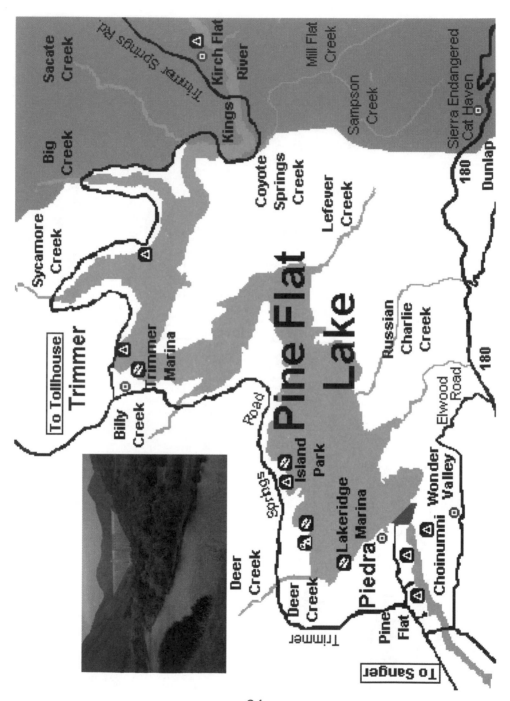

Sacate Creek

Big Creek

Kirch Flat

Kings River

Trimmer Springs Rd.

Mill Flat Creek

Sampson Creek

Sierra Endangered Cat Haven

Dunlap

180

Coyote Springs Creek

Lefever Creek

Sycamore Creek

Pine Flat Lake

To Tollhouse

Trimmer

Trimmer Marina

Russian Charlie Creek

Billy Creek

Elwood Road

180

Road

Springs

Island Park

Wonder Valley

Deer Creek

Lakeridge Marina

Choinumni

Deer Creek

Piedra

Trimmer

Pine Flat

To Sanger

Pine Flat Dam

Holding back the Kings River is a 429-foot tall structure that was completed in 1954. The lake is 20 miles long with 67 miles of shoreline. It provides flood control and irrigation benefits to the San Joaquin Valley.

A hydroelectric plant was completed in 1984. Visitors from near and far come to fish, water or jet ski, float around on a houseboat or just plain relax. Three public campgrounds are available on a first-come, first-served basis. Each is suitable for RV and tent camping.

There are two marinas on the lake, Deer Creek and Trimmer, offering boat and slip rentals, fuel, camping and fishing supplies. The Kings River, below the dam, is planted weekly. Fishing tackle, supplies and information are available at the marinas, as well as from several stores near the lake. Sightseers can enjoy scenic views of the lake from Trimmer Springs road and the observation area at the dam.

Picnic facilities are also available. Below the dam, the shady banks of the Kings River offer picnic sites and streamside walking trails. The Blue Oak Nature Trail, located at Island Park, offers a pleasant and informative walk.

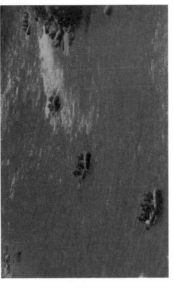

Group Camp Reservations
(559) 787-2589
Lakeridge Marina
(559) 787-2506
Trimmer Marina
(559) 855-2039
Trimmer Ranger Office
(559) 855-8321

65

Pinehurst Lodge - Highway 245
Gateway to Kings Canyon and Sequoia

(559) 336-2603
www.pinehurstlodge.com

When traveling to Kings Canyon or Sequoia along Highway 245, plan to stop here for a wonderful home cooked meal. In the cool fall and cold winters, there's always a warm fire in the old brick fireplace. You can stay the night and rest peacefully under the Sierra Nevada stars, perhaps use it as a base camp to explore the beautiful surroundings for a few days. Boyden Caves, Moro Rock, the Giant Forest, Cedar Grove and the awe inspiring Kings River running through the deep canyon are all spectacular places to visit. In the winter, you can play in the snow locally or drive over to Wolverton for cross country skiing or take a snowshoe hike in Sequoia.

GALIHER
MOUNTAIN
APPLES & PEARS
52775 HIGHWAY 245

66

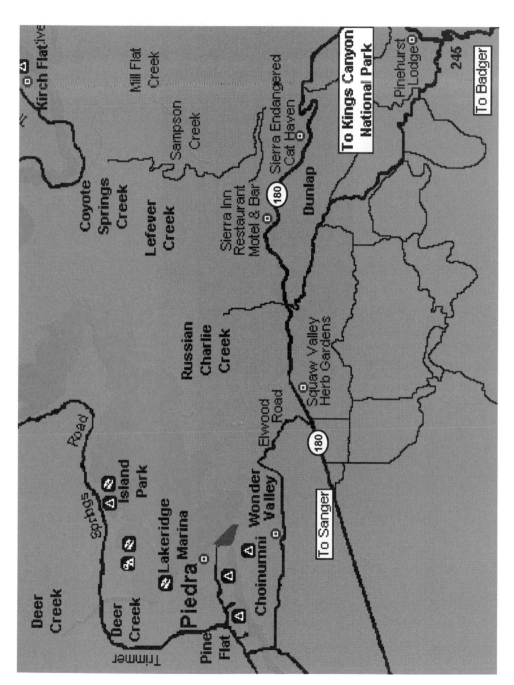

Prather

At the junction of Auberry Road and Highway 168 is a place to rest awhile and gather last minute supplies as you head up the hill. There's a supermarket, a gas station, a major drug store, a bakery, plus stores offering sporting goods, auto parts and livestock feed and tack.

Plan to have a meal while you're here. There are five good restaurants ready to satisfy your appetite.

ATM machines are available at the bank and in the Longs Drug Store. Lodging is available in Auberry. Two Indian Casinos are nearby if want to try your luck playing cards or with the slot machines. Good Luck!

To Shaver Lake
Tollhouse
To Pine Flat Lake
North Fork
Power House
Auberry
168
Lodge Road
Tollhouse
168
168
Prather
San Joaquin
Auberry Road
Millerton Rd
To Oakhurst
41
Millerton
Auberry Road
Copper
Road 211
To Madera
145
206
Friant
To Fresno

Reedley

Reedley is located in the central San Joaquin Valley portion of California, lying just inland between the State's coastal mountain ranges and the Sierra Nevada. Civil War hero Thomas Law Reed settled here to provide wheat for Gold Rush miners in the mid 1800's.

When mining faded, wheat demand slackened and water was diverted for crop irrigation, which lead to a tradition of bountiful field, tree, and vine fruit harvests.

An important element in the early town was a colony of German Mennonites, whose strong traditions and values still shape Reedley's culture.

Fishermen, water skiers, boaters, swimmers and picnickers find the scenic Kings River a paradise. The river runs right through the town's backyard, providing a natural beachfront setting.

There are several challenging golf courses to tempt you. Pine Flat Lake and Kings Canyon or Sequoia are within a hour's drive. In season, travel the Blossom Trail to see many of the colors Mother Nature provides. There are many fine places for lodging and great restaurants. Be sure to visit the Opera House and the Mennonite Quilting Center.

Reedley Tourism
(559) 638-3548
www.reedleychamber.org.

69

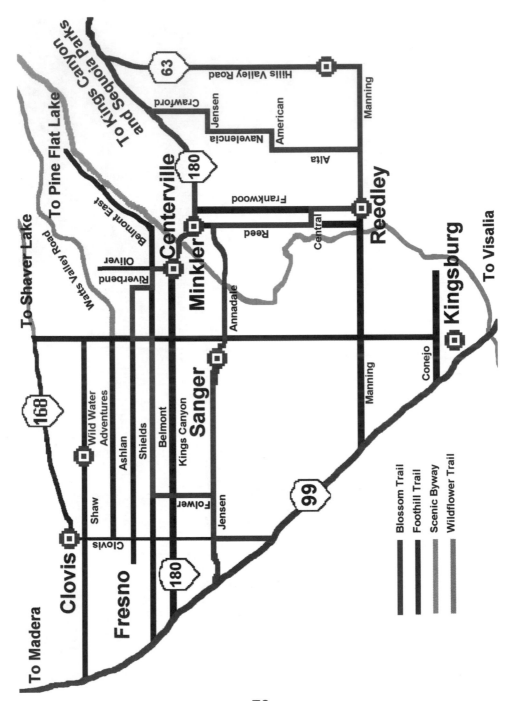

70

Sanger

Rich in history as a logging and agricultural center, Sanger is a gateway to many wonderful vacation spots. Pine Flat Lake, the Kings River and Wonder Valley Ranch are just minutes away.

Kings Canyon and Sequoia National Parks are just an hour up the road. The Sierra Endangered Cat Haven is interesting to visit, as is the Sanger Depot Museum with it's rich depiction of the town's history. All major services are available when you visit Sanger, "Home of the Nation's Christmas Tree!"

Sanger Chamber
(559) 576-4737
www.sanger.org.

San Joaquin River Parkway

Stretching from Friant Dam to the bridge on Highway 99, the River Parkway is a wonderful place to jog, skate or ride a horse or simply walk along this scenic river. There are many places to stop, rest or perhaps have a picnic. If you prefer, hop aboard a canoe or other non-motorized watercraft and travel along the river. The views are terrific!

You can fish in the river, just below the dam. It is stocked weekly and is a very popular spot. Swimming is a favorite activity in the Lost Lake Park. Camping is also available there. You can get supplies from the Lost Lake Store or from the small town of Friant. Gas is also available in Friant.

An abundance of migratory birds are found along the river. During the winter you can take a tour of Millerton State Park and see bald and golden eagles. A variety of other wildlife can be seen as well, like coyotes, bobcats, raccoons and rabbits .

72

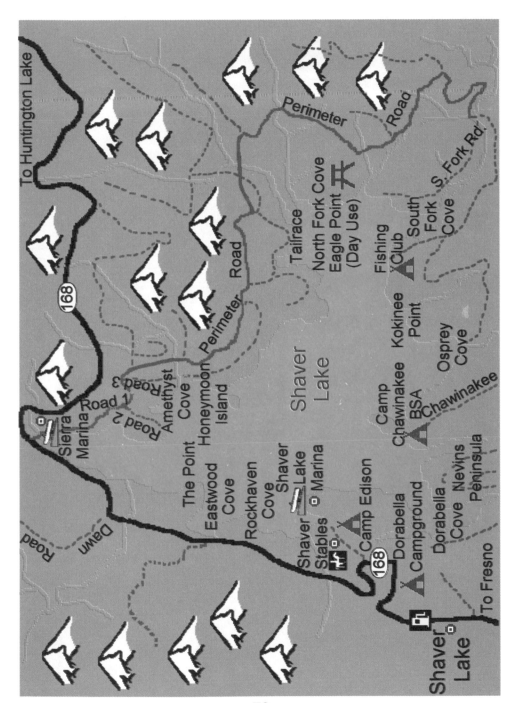

Shaver Lake

Year round events help make this recreational area a favorite spot to bring the family for some special time together. A fishing derby, a logger's jamboree and a car show are among the many activities the local citizens host annually. Naturally, all the regular activities a High Sierra resort town offers can be enjoyed here: fishing, camping, skiing, hiking and swimming. All services are available during your visit.

Around the Lake

Lodging and camping accommodations are varied at Shaver Lake. Camp Edison offers a year round place for those interested in camping. The local chamber has a line on the motels, lodges and bed & breakfast establishments in the area. Two marinas on the lake help you with your boating needs. Houseboat, jet ski, fishing boat and power boat rentals are available.

Each has a complete line of tackle and bait, as do the sporting good stores in the town of Shaver. You'll want to take time and visit the Shaver Historical Museum. Among other things, it depicts the Shaver Lake logging heritage. It's interesting to learn how logs were transported to the San Joaquin Valley in the early days!

Camp Edison
(559) 841-3810
www.campedison.com
Sierra Marina
(559) 841-3324
www.sierramarina.com
Shaver Lake Marina
(559) 841-5331

Shaver Stables

Bring the family in for a wonderful ride around the beautiful countryside.

If you would like to plan a pack trip into the backcountry, the knowledgeable staff at D&F Pack Station, just up the road at Huntington Lake, will assist you.

(559) 841-8500
www.highsierrapacker.com

75

Sierra Endangered Cat Haven

Located on Highway 180, in Dunlap, the Cat Haven is a very interesting and unique experience. The tour begins at the gift shop and takes about an hour. It is suggested you wear comfortable, sturdy walking shoes!

The quarter-mile walking tour is on a decomposed granite trail which is sloped in places. Strollers can be accommodated, but most folks prefer to backpack infants. If walking is difficult for you, or a member of your party, consider one of the in-door educational programs. The weather can be quite hot in the summer and fall, yet cold in the spring and winter. Dress accordingly for the season. It's always a good idea to wear a hat and use sunscreen.

The path is partially shaded and provides good exercise. There are no drinking fountains on the tour, so you'll probably want to carry a bottle of water with you.

Be sure to allow extra time to see the educational room and the gift shop.

May 1st to September 30th
9am to 6pm
October 1st to April 30th
9am to 4pm
Closed Wednesday
General admission is $5.75
Kids five to twelve years $3.25
Seniors 62 years and older $4.75
Children four and under enter free.

76

Squaw Valley Herb Gardens

Nestled along Highway 180, on the way to Kings Canyon Park, sits this beautiful herb garden. You can make advanced reservations to stop, have a tour, see a theater presentation, sample a tasting and really have a lovely time. You'll also be treated to work created by an artist that works with stone carvings that are very unique.

(559) 332-2909
www.squawvalleyherbgardens..com

Table Mountain Casino & Bingo

Situated on Millerton Road, equidistant from Clovis, Fresno, Madera and Oakhurst, this Indian gaming facility offers a lot to visitors. Among the many games you can choose to play are video poker, regular coin slot machines, Texas Hold em, Las Vegas style Blackjack and Bingo. You can even win a million dollars with just one pull of the handle!

When you get hungry, you're in luck! The popular Eagles Landing Restaurant serves up delicious meals. People drive for miles just to experience the wonderful cuisine. Whether your favorite meal is breakfast, lunch or dinner, you'll have lots of tasty items from which to choose. Naturally, like the casino, the restaurant is open round the clock. It's a great place to bring someone special for a fantastic evening.

A variety of entertainment is also presented by the casino. From sanctioned professional boxing matches, karate tournaments, musical concerts and a luxurious New Year's Eve party, the staff is always looking for new and exciting presentations for visitors. Don't forget to stop by the Gift Shop and browse through the interesting items, including Indian sculptures, artifacts and Southwestern jewelry.

See Maps Page 41 or 62
(559) 822-2485
(800) 541-3637

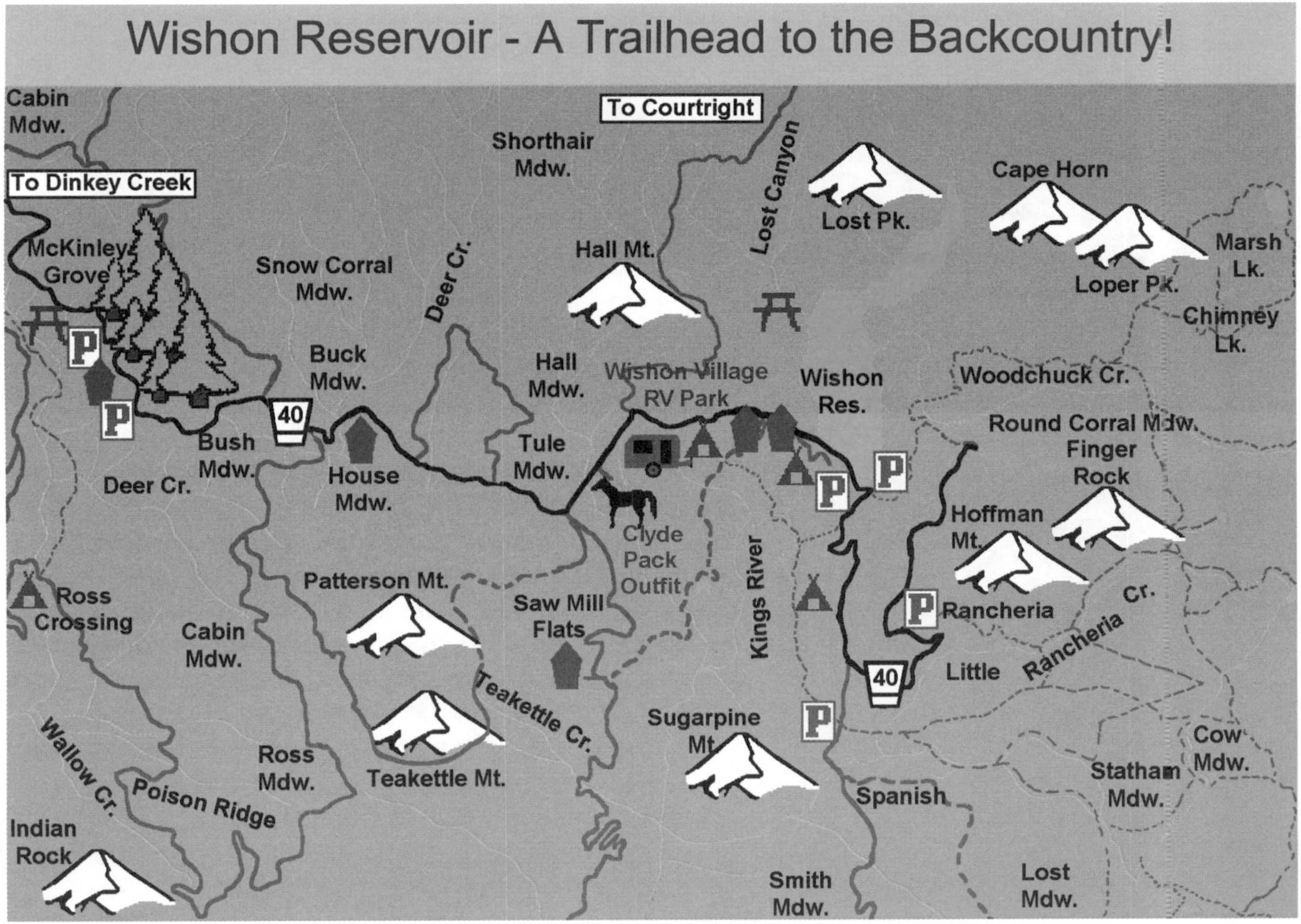

Wishon Reservoir - A Trailhead to the Backcountry!

To Courtright

To Dinkey Creek

Cabin Mdw.

Marsh Lk.

Chimney Lk.

Cape Horn

Loper Pk.

Lost Pk.

Woodchuck Cr.

Round Corral Mdw.

Finger Rock

Hoffman Mt.

Rancheria

Little Rancheria

Cow Mdw.

Statham Mdw.

Lost Mdw.

Lost Canyon

Wishon Res.

Wishon Village RV Park

Hall Mt.

Shorthair Mdw.

Hall Mdw.

Tule Mdw.

Clyde Pack Outfit

Kings River

Saw Mill Flats

Sugarpine Mt

Spanish

Smith Mdw.

40

Deer Cr.

Snow Corral Mdw.

Buck Mdw.

House Mdw.

Bush Mdw.

Patterson Mt.

Teakettle Cr.

Teakettle Mt.

40

Deer Cr.

Cabin Mdw.

Ross Mdw.

Poison Ridge

Ross Crossing

Wallow Cr.

Indian Rock

McKinley Grove

Wishon Reservoir is an easy 80 mile drive east of Fresno. The road is open from late May until the end of October. It is a gateway to a variety of back country adventures. Great fishing abounds in nearby lakes and streams. Hunt for deer or bear. Enjoy the many hiking, mountain biking and off-road trails nearby.

Enjoy drowning a few worms or drag enticing lures behind the boat to take a nice size German Brown or Rainbow Trout. Beautiful waterfalls cascade towards the reservoir and osprey fish for dinner as you cruise along. Take the family over to the pack station and saddle up to take a pleasant ride into the surrounding scenic forests.

A number of off-road trails emanate from Wishon. Permits for overnight stays are available from the Dinkey Creek Ranger Station. There is a general store, RV sites with full hookups, restrooms with hot showers and laundry facilities, campgrounds, boat rentals and docking facilities. Visit the friendly bar on weekend evenings. Be advised, no fuel is available here!

80

WONDER VALLEY
Family Camp

Now a peaceful spot, legend tells of colorful characters and violent times. The Yokut tribe made this their home in the 1800s. In 1891, this foothill retreat was a refuge for the notorious Dalton Brothers gang.

Their hideout was on "Dalton" mountain, at the valley's east end, where they kept a watchful eye out for any pursuit. Ranchers were the principal occupants here during the early 1900s. George Pierson began the guest ranch tradition by allowing friends to stay at his ranch and help with the cattle "for the fun of it." The Ranch is alive with many amenities, and close by are fishing, hiking and river rafting on the mighty Kings River. Sequoia and Kings Canyon Parks are just an hour's drive.

(800) 821-2801
www.wondervalley.com

81

Giant Sequoia National Monument

This recently designated area consists of two segments carved out of the Sequoia National Forest.

It was established to protect the trees and the watersheds in which they grow. It also serves as a reminder of the wasteful logging practices used a century ago.

Mature sequoia timber is very brittle. The giant trees often shattered upon impact when felled. Consequently, less than half the timber ever made it to the mills. Most just ended up being used as matchsticks, shingles, or grapestakes.

Converse Basin, once one of the world's largest sequoia groves, was logged between 1897 and 1907.

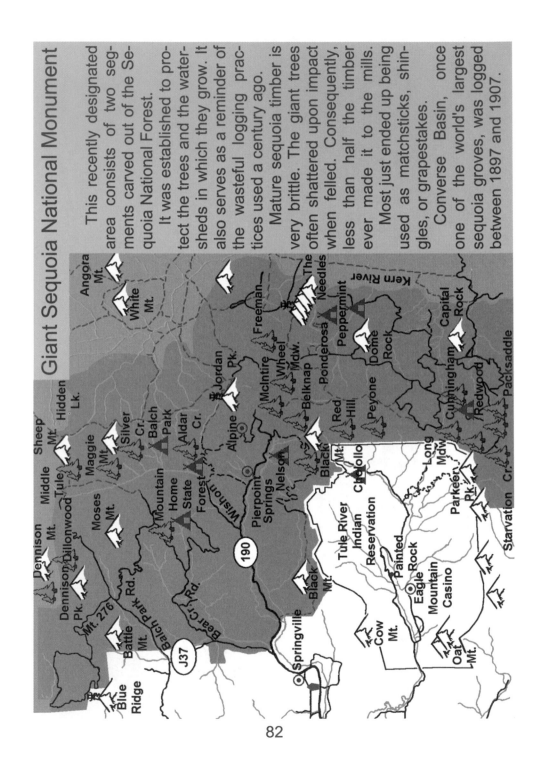

The poor logging techniques are most evident in Stump Meadow, which today is both beautiful and haunting. Here you see shattered trunks, rotting where they landed. Nearby is the General Noble Tree stump, nicknamed the Chicago Stump. It was cut for the 1893 World's Columbian Exposition in Chicago. Too big to transport, the tree's bark was segmented, then reassembled for display. Fairgoers actually thought it was a hoax.

Access the northern portion from 180 north of Grant Grove in Kings Canyon National Park, go past McGee Overlook, turn west on gravel Forest Road 13S03, and continue 2 miles to F.R. 13S66. To reach the southern section, take 190 east from Porterville.

There are many places in the Monument to enjoy backcountry camping, fishing, hiking as well as sightseeing.

Lodging, dining and basic supplies are available in the National Parks and surrounding communities.

Be aware that motor vehicle fuel is **NOT** available in in Sequoia or Kings Canyon National Parks. It is available in the communities outside the parks.

This is an excellent place for families to spend time together. Check out the following pages.

83

Balch Park

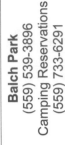

Deep in the Sierra Nevada, this county park is a gem. It sits among giant sequoias, and is very popular with its two ponds stocked with trout every week during the season.

There's a museum, barbecue facilities, 71 campsites, playground, and modern restrooms. On Saturday evenings, take the family to the amphitheatre where the Rangers give an interesting presentation.

You are surrounded by the Sequoia National Park, and very close to King's Canyon National Park. Each offers a variety of day activities for folks of all ages. The area is very photogenic.

A number of hiking trails are in the area for day hikes or extended stays. If you plan to stay overnight in the wilderness, you will need a permit from the local ranger.

If you would like to go horseback riding, or perhaps are interested in a backcountry pack trip, go over and see the folks at the Balch Park Pack Station. They can assist you with hourly rides, wilderness camping and fishing trips, or suggest hunting trips during the relevant seasons.

Balch Park
(559) 539-3896
Camping Reservations
(559) 733-6291
Balch Park Pack Station
(559) 539-2227
www.balchpark.com

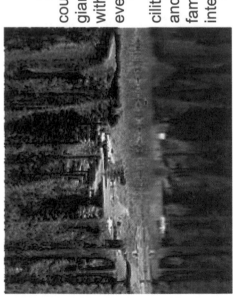

Camp Nelson

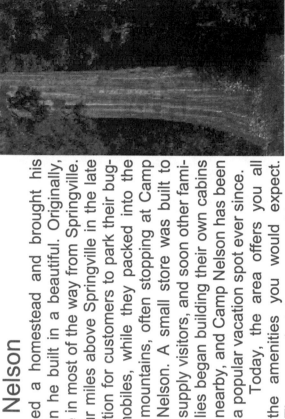

In 1886, John Nelson obtained a homestead and brought his daughters to the split shake cabin he built in a beautiful. Originally, visitors had to ride a horse or hike in most of the way from Springville. A pack station was built about four miles above Springville in the late 1890s. There was room at the station for customers to park their buggies or wagons, and later automobiles, while they packed into the mountains, often stopping at Camp Nelson. A small store was built to supply visitors, and soon other families began building their own cabins nearby, and Camp Nelson has been a popular vacation spot ever since.

Today, the area offers you all the amenities you would expect. There are hotel rooms, cabins, an RV park and nearby camping. Good food, necessary supplies and great activities are available. Motor vehicle fuel is sold in Ponderosa and Springville, just minutes away.

A short distance from the lodge, is a trail that crosses mountain streams and passes giant Sequoias. It takes a couple of hours down and three hours up. It is well worth the effort, but from the lodge you can hike a short distance on the trail and see some beautiful sites. From the lodge go east on Nelson until the road ends at the trailhead.

Camping Reservations
(877) 444-6777
www.reserveusa.com
**Camp Nelson General
Store & RV Park**
(559) 542-3700
Camp Nelson Lodge
(559) 542-0904
www.campnelsonlodge.com
Cedar Slope Inn
(559) 542-2319
Golden Trout Wilderness Packtrains
(559) 542-2816
www.goldentroutpacktrains.com
Camping Reservations
(877) 444-6777
www.reserveusa.com
Pierpoint Lodge
(559) 542-2423
www.pierpointsprings.com

Ponderosa

Along Highway 190, this beautiful area is accessible year round. Most of the time you can enjoy the surroundings in your vehicle, on foot or aboard a horse. But in the winter, it's time to get a set of cross country skis or some snowshoes to view the scenery.

There are excellent facilities for you and the family. Services and motor vehicle fuel are available.

The area is close to many interesting trails. Take the Freeman Creek Trail to see some big trees. It's two to three miles in, all downhill, so the climb back is steep. The Trail of the 100 Giants is great for the family. You wander through a grove of ancient sequoias on an easy 1/2-mile loop. Trailhead parking is 11 miles south of Ponderosa Lodge on 190. If you get a chance, drive to the Stagg Tree trail and walk around it. There are some small but very pretty water falls nearby.

Dome Rock is another place to try and visit. It's a favorite with amateur astronomers and it is just a two mile drive south of Ponderosa on 190. Go to road 21S69. It's a short hike to the top of Dome Rock. You can see the Kern Canyon 3000 feet below, the giant granite needles, and Lake Isabella.

Tule River

The Tule River is the most southern of the all-year-running rivers that flow directly west from the crests of the Sierra Nevada. Its three major forks, North, Middle, and South, drain some 400 square miles of higher mountains and lower hills.

The North and Middle Forks join at Springville continuing to Success Dam, where the South Fork joins it. The Upper Tule River area has been very popular as a tourist destination for years.

River rafting, fishing, hiking, mountain biking, horseback riding and just enjoying the sheer beauty of the area attract new and repeat travelers.

Be sure to visit the Quaking Aspens. They are particularly beautiful trees with white, birch-like bark. Their name derives from their tendency to shimmer in the sunlight.

The leaves of these trees, which reach heights of 70 feet, are a lighter color on one side than on the other. When the wind blows the leaves give the entire tree a shimmering appearance. Due to this and other elements in the scenic forest, be sure to always carry your camera, and plenty of film!

Camping Reservations
(877) 444-6777
www.reserveusa.com
Friends of the Tule River
(559) 539-8401
Slate Mountain Resort
(559) 542-1900
Tule River Ranger Station
(559) 539-2607
Upper Tule Association
(559) 542-2551

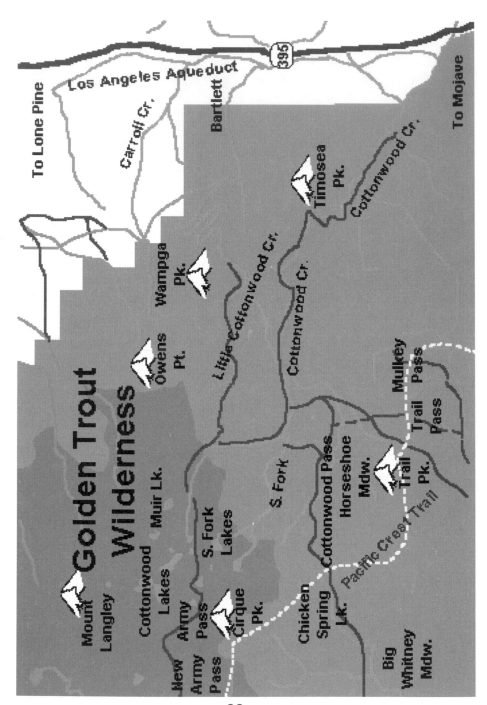

Golden Trout Wilderness totals 303,511 acres. It was created in 1978 and is named after the brightly colored California state fish, the golden trout, that lives in relative abundance in the waters of the area. Naturally, fishing is a popular past time, especially fly fishing.

There are special restrictions that apply to anglers, make sure you know what they are. Golden Trout Wilderness is a large drainage basin surrounded by high, jagged peaks. It dominates much of the western Sequoia National Forest, with its eastern

section in Inyo National Forest. Piñon-pine woodlands rise to extensive Jeffrey pine forest and meadows at mid elevations. Red fir, lodgepole pines and foxtail pines are at higher elevations before hitting the timberline. Two wild and scenic rivers, the North and South Forks of the Kern River, flow across the area. The North Fork rages through stunningly beautiful country and offers one of America's premier multiday white-water adventures, a challenge for the most expert rafter. Summer thunderstorms are common, but water may be scarce away from the rivers during dry spells.

About 150 miles of exceptionally scenic back packing and horsepacking trails transverse the area. Stock forage is plentiful after the first of July. The Pacific Crest Trail follows parts of the eastern edge of the area and the Cottonwood Pass Trail crosses it to the west. The views are wonderful.

You'll want to get a wilderness permit, which is required to enter the back country in most areas.

Keep in mind that all bikes and motorized vehicles are prohibited in all wilderness areas. Pets and firearms are not permitted in wilderness areas.

There are four main points used to enter the Wilderness. Each has complete information and maps on the specific trails you may want to travel. Their numbers are listed be-

Sequoia National Forest (559) 784-1500 Mt. Whitney Ranger District (760) 876-6200	Tule River Ranger District (559) 539-2607 Cannell Meadow Ranger District (760) 376-3781

low. If you don't have your own livestock, there are good pack outfits in the area to assist you in planning an exciting trip into a camping and fishing paradise. Bring your camera!

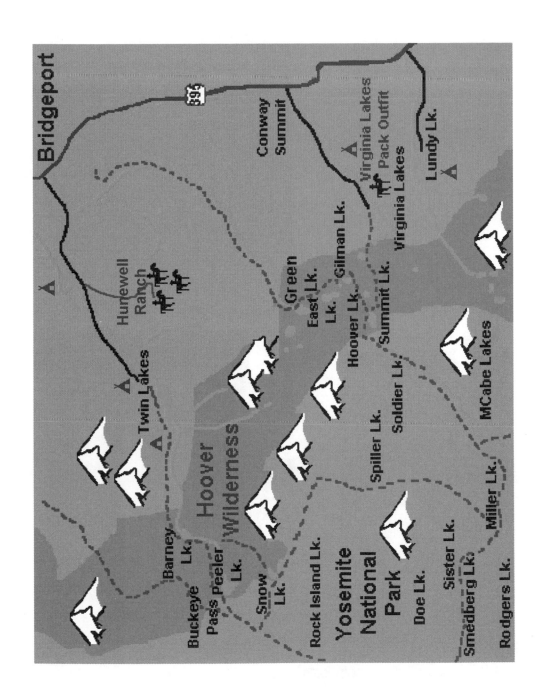

Bridgeport

Conway
Summit

Virginia Lakes

Virginia Lakes
Pack Outfit

Virginia Lakes

Lundy Lk.

Gilman Lk.

Green

East Lk.

Lk.

Hoover Lk.

Summit Lk.

Soldier Lk.

Spiller Lk.

MCabe Lakes

Hunewell
Ranch

Twin Lakes

Hoover

Wilderness

Barney
Lk.

Pass Peeler
Lk.

Buckeye

Snow
Lk.

Rock Island Lk.

Yosemite

National

Park

Doe Lk.

Sister Lk.

Smedberg Lk.

Miller Lk.

Rodgers Lk.

Hoover Wilderness

Established as a Primitive area in 1931, this became one of the original Wilderness Area members. Here is an extremely rugged and magnificently scenic area with elevations from around 8,000 feet to more than 12,000 feet, a region of alpine lakes and lovely meadows but little timber. It has a total of 48,601 acres.

The scarcity of firewood has resulted in a ban on wood fires in the very popular 20 Lakes Basin. Rainbow, brook, and golden trout inhabit the lakes. If you travel with stock, you should pack in all your feed. You may see cattle and sheep grazing, as some permits were issued to ranchers prior to designation.

The presence of black bears should encourage you to hang your food at night. Rain, snow, strong winds, and bitter cold can occur in all seasons. Hoover and Yosemite share a common border. Permits are required to hike into the park. The area, with its well-maintained trail system, receives heavy human use. You'll encounter the least human traffic in the northern portion. You can obtain a Wilderness Permit from the Ranger Units below.

Mammoth Lakes Ranger District
Visitors Center
(760) 934-5200
Lee Vining Ranger District
(760) 845-5743
Bridgeport Ranger District
(760) 843-4837

Inyo County and the Sierra

Come visit 15 of California's Historical Landmarks, enjoy great fishing, skiing, camping, lodging, fine food, museums, hiking, horseback riding and more!

You can hike up Mt. Whitney, the highest peak in contiguous United States. It's a short drive to Death Valley, the lowest point in the U.S!

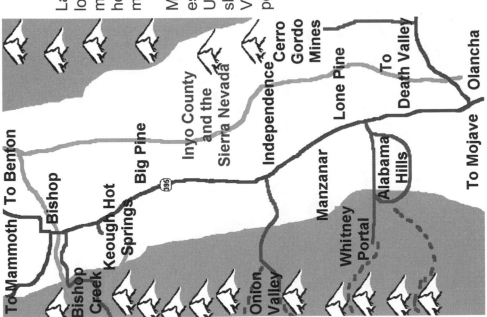

To Mammoth / To Benton
Bishop
Bishop Creek
Keough Hot Springs
Big Pine
Inyo County and the Sierra Nevada
Onion Valley
Independence
Cerro Gordo Mines
Lone Pine
Manzanar
Whitney Portal
Alabama Hills
To Death Valley
To Mojave
Olancha
395

Inyo boasts a host of outdoor activities and interesting things to see, like pack trips, visiting one of many museums, hiking along mountain streams and observing local cactus.

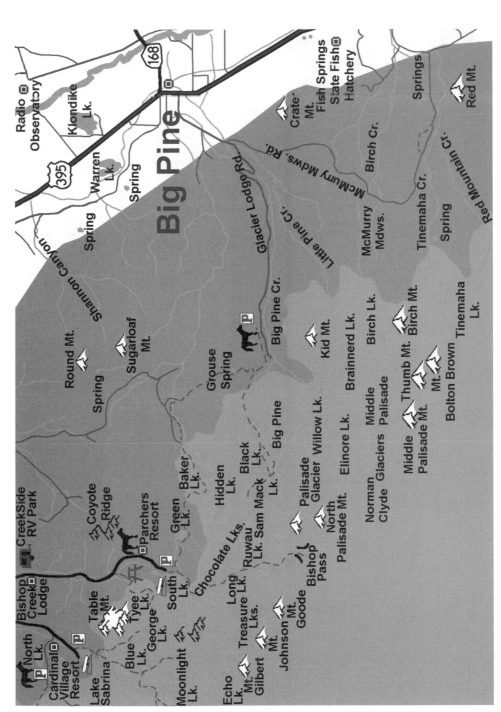

Big Pine

168
395

Radio Observatory
Klondike Lk.

Warren Lk.
Spring
Spring

Shannon Canyon

Round Mt.
Spring

Sugarloaf Mt.
Spring

Grouse Spring

Glacier Lodge Rd.

Little Pine Cr.

Big Pine Cr.

Crater Mt.
Fish Springs State Fish Hatchery
Springs

Birch Cr.

McMurry Mdws. Rd.

McMurry Mdws.

Tinemaha Cr.
Spring

Red Mountain Cr.

Red Mt.

Kid Mt.

Brainnerd Lk.
Birch Lk.
Birch Mt.

Middle Palisade
Thumb Mt.
Bolton Brown Mt.
Tinemaha Lk.

Norman Clyde Glaciers
Middle Palisade Mt.

Palisade Glacier
Willow Lk.
North Palisade Mt.
Elinore Lk.

Big Pine

Black Lk.
Sam Mack Lk.
Ruwau Lk.

Hidden Lk.

Baker Lk.
Green Lk.

Chocolate Lks.
Treasure Lks.
Long Lk.

Bishop Pass
Goode Mt.

Johnson Mt.

Gilbert Mt.
Echo Lk.

Moonlight Lk.

Table Mt.
Tyee Lks.
George Lk.
South Lk.
Blue Lk.
Lake Sabrina

North Lk.
Cardinal Village Resort

Bishop Creek Lodge
CreekSide RV Park
Coyote Ridge
Parchers Resort

95

Big Pine

The "Small Town, with the Big Back Yard"! Things to explore around the area are diverse and numerous. There's plenty of camping, lodging and RV Parks to serve as a "home" base. This is a photographer's and sportsman paradise.

Residents and visitors alike are lured into the ageless canyons and mountains surrounding the town. See the Ancient Bristlecone Forest and Palisade Glacier.

Fish the Owens River or any of the trout laden lakes that are close by in Big Pine Canyon. Slip over to Death Valley and see what that historical area has to offer. Horsepack trips are popular and a great family adventure. If you don't have your own livestock, there are packers in the area to serve you. Many off-road trails await you. There are hot springs to soak in. Westgard Pass takes you to the Eureka Sand Dunes, the tallest dunes in the Great Basin, with some shifting piles of sand reaching 900 feet in height! See old rock dwellings, mines and prospector's shacks along the way. If you like bird watching, you'll flock here to see Great Blue Herons, American White Pelicans, bald eagles, ferruginous hawks, yellow billed cuckoos and mountain bluebirds. Rock collectors also thrill to the findings they experience in the area.

Big Pine Chamber
(760) 938-2114
Owens ValleyRadio Observatory Tour
(760) 938-2075
Camp Reservations
(877) 444-6777
Glacier Pack Train
(760) 938-2538

96

Eastern Sierra Gateway!

Bishop is a wonderful place to spend several days, if possible! A variety of motels, bed and breakfast establishments and camping facilities are available to you during your visit. Many fine restaurants offer a variety of fare for your dining pleasure.

You can try your luck at the Paiute Indian Casino, play a round of golf, go bowling or perhaps you'd like to take in a movie.

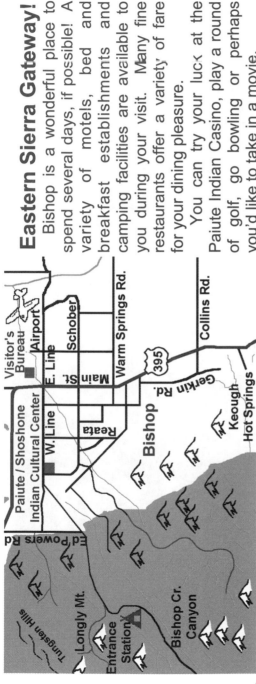

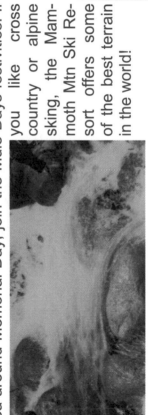

You'll want to visit the Laws Railroad Museum and Historical Site, plus the Paiute Shoshone Indian Cultural Center. Fly fishing is excellent in the Bishop area. Several guides are available to teach you the skill or lead you to the best spots! Horseback riding and pack trips are available from a variety of pack stations. If you're in the area around Memorial Day, join the Mule Days festivities. If you like cross country or alpine skiing, the Mammoth Mtn Ski Resort offers some of the best terrain in the world!

The Mono Craters, part of the volcanic history of the area are an easy drive, and an interesting spot to view. Mono Lake is world famous, with its tufas, an abundance of migratory birds, and incredible majesty. Take a lunch, tour the Mono Lake Visitor's Center and be sure to bring along your camera.

The Hot Springs Creek area is another you'll want to view. It includes a Fish Hatchery, that you can tour, plus hot mineral springs in which you can relax.

What ever you enjoy doing during your vacation, rest assured you can find it the Bishop area

Bishop Area Visitors Bureau
(760) 873-8405
www.bishopvisitor.com

98

Bishop Creek Canyon

The entrance to the canyon is only nine miles from Bishop. Great fishing, camping, hiking and horseback riding trails are waiting for you. The road is open during the late spring and summer months. It closed in winter due to snow. Backpackers can park in one of the several designated trailhead parking lots. There are eight fee camp sites in the canyon. The South Fork of Bishop Creek is dotted with many great fishing and hiking destinations. South Lake is 23 miles up the canyon and is a very popular trailhead that leads to a variety of back country hiking spots. Other places to visit are Brown and Green Lakes trails, the Bishop Pass Trail, the Treasure Lakes Trail, the Chocolate Lakes Trail and the Tyee Lakes Trail.

Camping Reservations
(877) 444-6777
Canyon Entrance Station
(760) 873– 2527
Bishop Creek Lodge
(760) 873-4484
Parchers Resort
(760) 873-4177

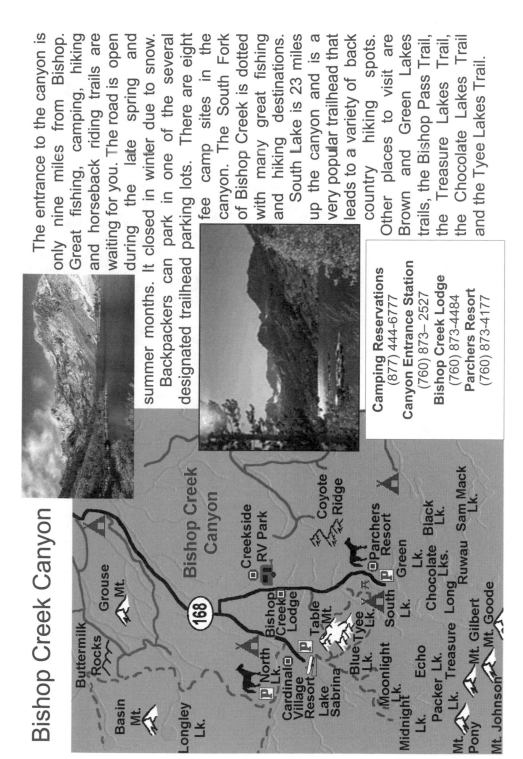

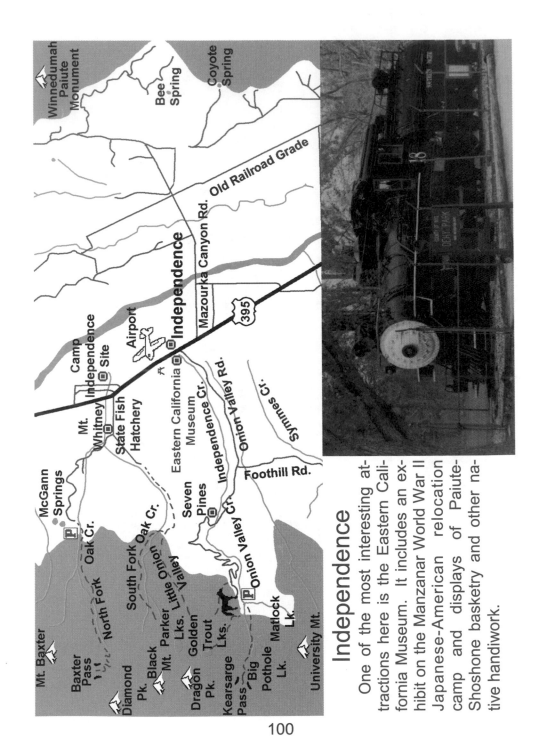

Independence

One of the most interesting attractions here is the Eastern California Museum. It includes an exhibit on the Manzanar World War II Japanese-American relocation camp and displays of Paiute-Shoshone basketry and other native handiwork.

You'll also see a reconstructed pioneer village, with early farm and mining equipment. The museum has an extensive photo collection and a library of local history.

Another local historical item is at Dehy Park. It is an old railroad locomotive. The Inyo County Courthouse is an impressive old building along Highway 395. County business is still conducted here.

You can ask for directions to see what is left of Camp Independence. It was established in 1862 to protect Owens Valley settlers from Indian attacks. About 200 soldiers arrived on the 4th of July, thus the camp was named!

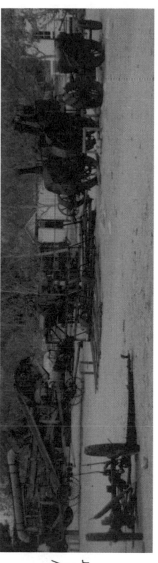

At the right and on the next few pages are pictures of many of the old items and a part of the Pioneer Village that you can see at the Eastern California Museum!

The Kearsarge Pass, once an Indian trading route, is close to town. It gives access to the John Muir Wilderness. There are a variety of roads leading to smaller trails that will lead you into the high country for great fishing, camping, sightseeing, hiking and horseback riding.

101

The Eastern California Museum
Is a wonderfully historical place
to spend at least an afternoon!

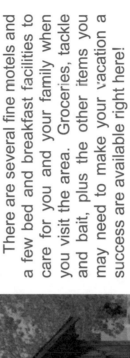

There are several fine motels and a few bed and breakfast facilities to care for you and your family when you visit the area. Groceries, tackle and bait, plus the other items you may need to make your vacation a success are available right here!

Eastern California Museum
(760) 874-8473
Independence Chamber
(760) 878-0084
Onion Valley Pack Station
(760) 387-2797

Keough Hot Springs

Located just seven miles south of Bishop, the hot springs have a strong history. The mineral waters were a favorite spot and were basically used for medicinal and healing purposes by the Indians and then the settlers in the area. During the 1920s and 30s, it was a complete health and leisure resort. It was a central point of celebration on holidays for all of Owens Valley. Barbecues, fireworks, dancing, fishing and comfortable lodging were the highlights. Movie stars and other famous people can to the springs every year. Let the owners tell you all the stories that lie behin the scenes! So be sure to stop and visit at the hot springs when you travel through the area.

Keough Hot Springs
(760) 872-4670
www.keoughhotsprings.com

Lone Pine - In Mt. Whitney's Shadow

Famous around the world for this "chunk of granite", Lone Pine also features other awe inspiring attractions. Many of the old ,and new, westerns have been filmed just up the road at Alabama Hills. Manzanar, the World War II Japanese-American relocation camp is near by.

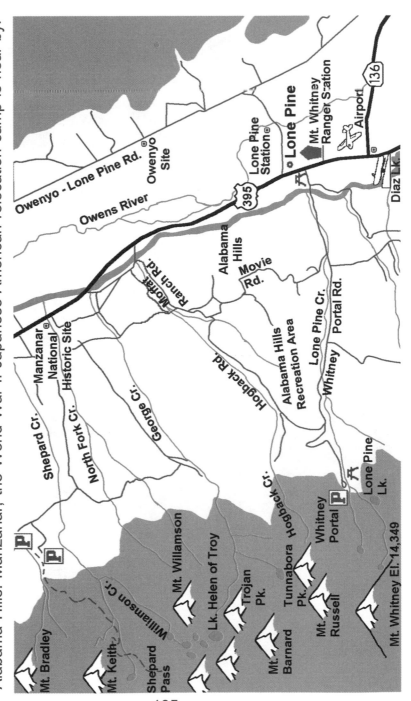

105

If you run out of things to do, you can visit the Interagency Visitor's Center at the Junction of Highway 395 and 136, the road to Death Valley. Lodging, supplies, good food and all major services are available to you in Lone Pine. This is a wonderful place for folks of all ages to spend some time. Be sure to bring your golf clubs as well as your fishing pole and hiking boots.

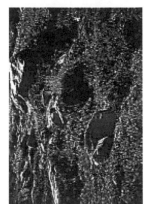

Lone Pine Chamber
(760) 876-4444

Manzanar - Japanese Relocation Camp

Once a thriving pear and apple growing center, Manzanar is best known for being one of 10 camps where Japanese-American citizens were interned during World War II. Construction on the camp began in 1942. It remained in operation until late in 1945. At its peak, Manzanar had a population of nearly 10,000 people. The facility covered 6,000 acres, including the camp, an adjacent agricultural site, a reservoir, airport, cemetery and sewage treatment plant. About 550 acres were used to house the various temporary visitors and many administrative facilities.

It was enclosed by barbed wire and secured by guard towers. Few of the camp's buildings remain today. Among those remaining is the camp auditorium, a large wooden frame building. A significant number of artifacts associated with the facility can be seen at the Eastern California Museum, located in Independence, about five miles north of the camp. You can take a self tour. Manzanar is just off U.S. Highway 395, 12 miles north of Lone Pine and close to Independence.

There are no facilities or water at this Historic Site. Use common sense and be aware of safety hazards.

107

Mt. Whitney - Highest in the Lower 48!

Climbing the mountain is a favorite of many outdoor folks. Mt. Whitney is just under 12 miles by foot from the Whitney Portal area. Whitney Portal is a 13 mile drive from Lone Pine.

Most hikers, aiming for the summit, take three days to achieve their goal. The first day, you leave Whitney Portal, with your camping gear and sufficient food and water for the three day period.

The first day's stop is Trail Camp, with an elevation of 12,000. After a good night's rest, you leave early the next morning. You leave your camp gear at Trail Camp. You'll reach the summit by noon and be back in time for bed! When you reach the top, it's time to enjoy the view, eat lunch and take a few pictures.

You spend the second night back at Trail Camp, with your return to Whitney Portal the next day around noontime. However, many serious backpackers can be at the summit by lunchtime, straight from Whitney Portal and back by evening. If you attempt this method, be sure to take a good jacket and plenty of high energy snacks and water. Do not drink stream water without treating it first.

The best time to visit the summit is from July through September. Almost all other times of the year, there is too much

Wilderness Reservations
(888) 374-3773
(760) 938-1136
Mt. Whitney Ranger District
(760) 876-6200

108

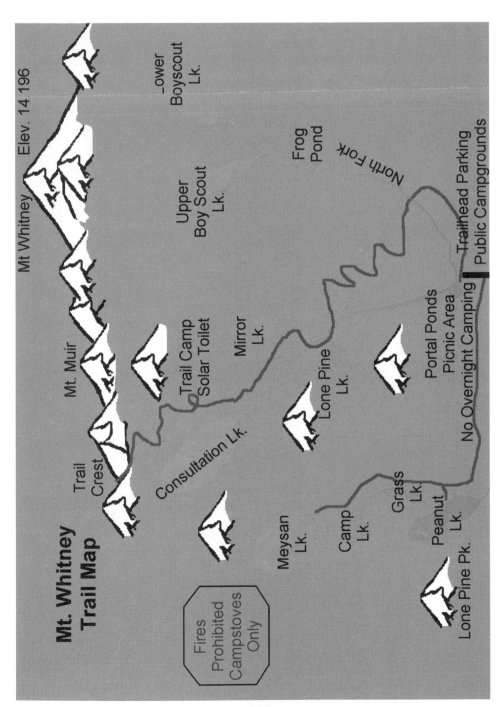

Mt. Whitney
Trail Map

Fires Prohibited Campstoves Only

Mt Whitney   Elev. 14 196

Lower Boyscout Lk.

Mt. Muir

Trail Crest

Upper Boy Scout Lk.

Frog Pond

North Fork

Trail Camp Solar Toilet

Mirror Lk.

Consultation Lk.

Lone Pine Lk.

Portal Ponds Picnic Area

Trailhead Parking
Public Campgrounds

No Overnight Camping

Meysan Lk.

Camp Lk.

Grass Lk.

Peanut Lk.

Lone Pine Pk.

Whitney Portal National Recreation Trail - Inyo National Forest

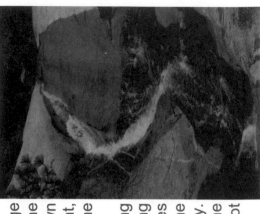

This is a designated National Recreation Trail and should not be confused with the strenuous trail up to Mt. Whitney's summit. There are two trailheads. The lower trailhead is at Lone Pine Campground, off Whitney Portal Road. The upper trailhead is at Whitney Portal near the fishing pond. The trail is about 4 miles long with the upper portion being in trees and canyon shade while traveling along the creek. The lower section is more open and can be very hot in the summer.

The elevation at the lower trailhead is 5,640 feet and the upper trailhead is 8,360 feet. Early morning travel is better. There are spectacular views of Mt. Whitney and the Alabama Hills, Owens Valley and the Inyo/White Mountains to the east.

From Whitney Portal Pond, cross the bridge by the restroom. There is a gradual decline along Lone Pine Creek. Rainbow and Brown Trout are present in the stream at this point, along with Eastern Brook Trout further down the trail in the Meysan Creek area.

The upper trail passes through a rock grotto before reaching Whitney Portal Campground. You will see many interesting rock formations and good views of the stream as it cascades towards the Owens Valley. Portons of the trail follow one of the original routes to the top of Mt. Whitney from the Owens Valley. Camping is not allowed, but campgrounds are in the area. The trail is for foot traffic only. Livestock is not allowed. Fires are not permitted.

110

Onion Valley Trails - Inyo National Forest

Venture into the backcountry, where hungry trout, beautiful scenery and solitude await you. Wilderness permits, required for all overnight hikes, are available at the Ranger Stations in Bishop and Lone Pine. This is bear territory, so proper food storage is required by federal law. Onion Valley is 15 miles west of Independence, take Market St., west off Highway 395.

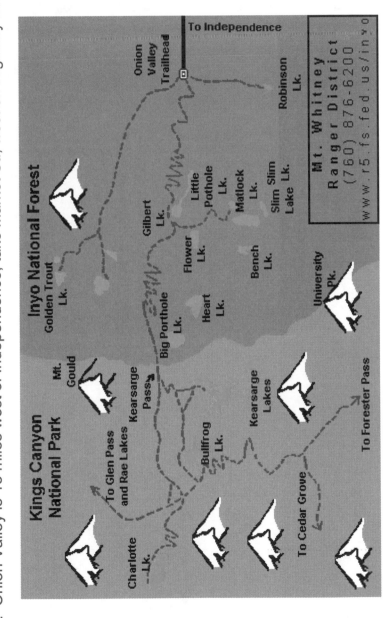

The Owens Valley Paiute originally controlled a vast area along the Owens River in what is now called Eastern California. This area is nestled between the majestic Sierra Nevada on the west and the White mountains on the east. The Bishop Paiute Tribe was created in 1912, with lands set aside for the Bishop colony, where Tribal members made their livelihood from farming and ranching.

In 1937, Congress ceded all previously owned Indian Lands to the City of Los Angeles in exchange for 1,391 acres of city-owned land.

This land exchange changed the way of life for Tribal members. The Tribe had to look for other means of income such as land leasing and most recently a gaming concession.

Today, exciting gaming action is waiting for you at the Paiute Palace Casino, with over 300 video gaming machines, Bingo, Poker and Palace 21 card tables.

After a day's activities in the surrounding area, treat yourself to a delicious meal while listening to live music or play your favorite game, non-stop to the early hours of the morning.

Be sure to stop by during your Sierra Nevada vacation, and take advantage of treating yourself to good time and a chance to win big.

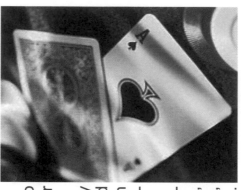

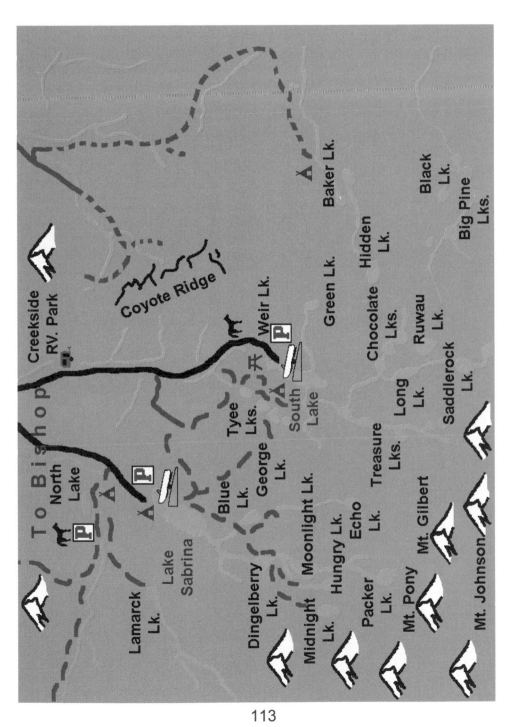

113

Lake Sabrina

Located on the middle fork of Bishop Creek, and surrounded by inspiring, 13,000' granite peaks, with glaciers on the rock faces, this area is very popular with hikers. It is a trailhead for a variety of places in the John Muir Wilderness. There is no overnight camping at trailhead parking sites.

When in Bishop on 395, turn west on West Line St. The lake is about 20 miles southwest of town. Follow the signs to the Bishop Creek Canyon Entrance, where you can get any necessary permits for back country travel. Build campfires only in designated steel fireplaces provided by the Forest Service. Rock fire rings are not permitted. Dead and down wood may be gathered from the ground, but use of wood from standing dead or live trees and shrubs is prohibited.

You may wish to purchase firewood at a canyon resort. The fishing is fantastic from boats or along the shoreline. Horseback riding is available locally!

Boating
Camping
Fishing
Hiking
Saddle Rides
Sightseeing
Swimming

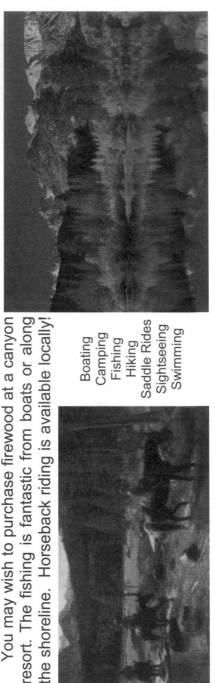

114

South Lake

At 10,000 ft., this lake presents a breathtaking scene and is loaded with trout. Meandering along beautiful Bishop Creek, the lake road is lined with pine, aspen and cottonwoods. This is a great place for a family vacation. Campgrounds, boat rentals, food services, lodging, pack trips and horseback riding are available.

This is also a popular jump off point with hikers and backpackers, with the trailhead for Bishop Pass leading to hundreds of scenic high-mountain lakes in the John Muir Wilderness. There is a full tackle shack with sodas, snacks, beer, fishing advice, tackle and maybe a few tall tales. There's a full marina with 14-foot alum num boat rentals with motors and private mooring facilities.

South Lake has rapidly become one of the most popular fishing lakes in the Eastern High Sierra. Local resort owners sponsor a very aggressive rearing and stocking program, and thus South Lake has a large population of trout, including big Alpers rainbows and Brown Trout. Several "Trophy Trout" have been taken from the lake in recent years.

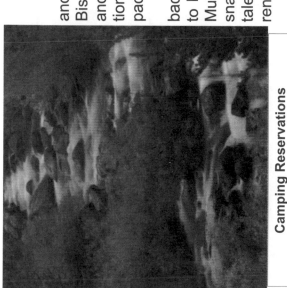

Camping Reservations
(800) 283-CAMP
Bishop Creek Lodge
(760) 873-4484
Parcher's Resort
(760) 873-4177
Lake Sabrina
(760) 873-7425
South Lake
(760) 873-4177
Bishop Pack Outfit
(760) 873-4785
White Mountain Ranger District
(760) 873-2500

The county is a great outdoor playground for millions of visitors annually. This massive forest extends for 165 miles along the California and Nevada border, covering nearly 2 million acres.

Here you'll find pristine lakes, high elevation meadows, winding streams, rugged peaks and the Great Basin Mountains. Elevations range from 4,000 feet in the Owens Valley to 14, 495 feet at Mt. Whitney, the highest peak in the continental U.S.

Inyo is thought to be a Native American name meaning "the dwelling place of the great spirit."

Several visitor centers throughout the forest provide information for your visit, one of the best is the Eastern Sierra Interageny Visitor Center at the junction of U.S. 395 and S.R. 136, one mile south of Lone Pine. Here are exhibits, maps, books and brochures on the area.

Inyo National Forest

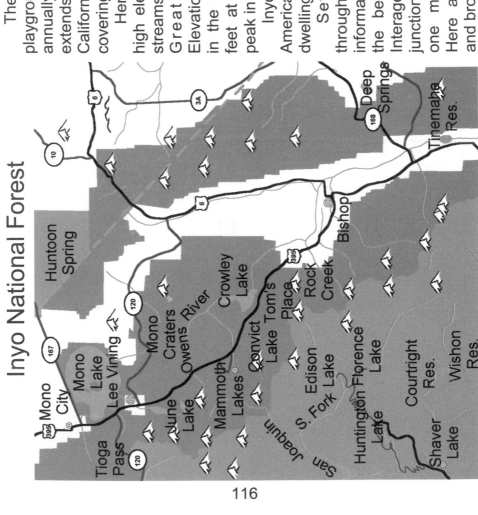

You can hike the Whitney Portal National Recreation Trail and Mt. Whitney Trail. There is a 4.6 mile trail that climbs 2,300 feet along the Lone Pine Creek drainage to Whitney Portal. From here is a 10.7 mile Mt. Whitney trail that takes hikers to the peak at 14,495 feet, so they can say they've climbed the highest mountain in the lower 48 states!

Visit the Ancient Bristlecone Pine Forest and Scenic Byway; the Big Pine Canyon and the Palisades Glacier; Bishop Creek Canyon with it's great fishing and hiking. Tour Rock Creek Canyon, Crowley Lake, the Owens River Valley, the Hot Creek Fish Hatchery and Hot Springs. Drop down into Red's Meadows with Sotcher Lake and the beavers, then see the Devil's Postpile formation.

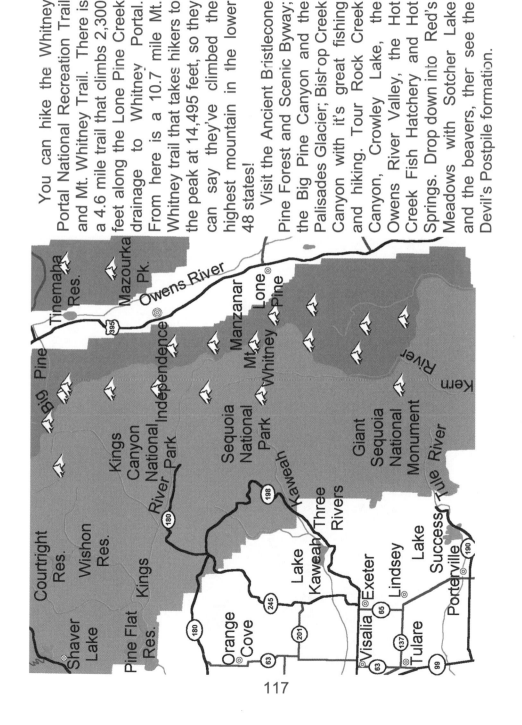

117

The Mammoth Lakes Basin features year round recreational activities; and Convict Lake, one of the most spectacular lakes and camping spots in the Sierra is a popular trailhead to the John Muir Wilderness. Next, is the June Lake Loop, featuring June, Grant, Silver and Gull Lakes, with wonderful campsites, good fishing and diverse geography. Up the road apiece is the Lee Vining Canyon Scenic Byway, the Tioga Pass Recreation area and Mono Lake.

Plan to spend a day at Mono Lake and the surrounding Mono Craters geothermal area. The Visitors Center at Mono Lake is a must! There are several interesting museums for you to tour along the way!

Most camp sites are available on a first-come, first-served basis. You can get supplies, fuel, bait, tackle and other items in most of the spots listed above. There are a variety of lodging facilities and numerous places to eat.

Check local areas for special promotions or one of the interesting annual events that occur.

Always travel safely and take your time.

Camping Reservations
(877) 444-6777
Eastern Sierra
Interageny Visitor Center
(760) 876-6222
Mt. Whitney Ranger District
(760) 876-6200
www.r5.fs.fed.us/Inyo
Bishop District Office
(760) 876-6200
Mammoth Ranger District
(760) 934-5500
Mono Basin Visitor Center
(760)647-3044
Mono Lake Ranger District
(760) 647-3000

118

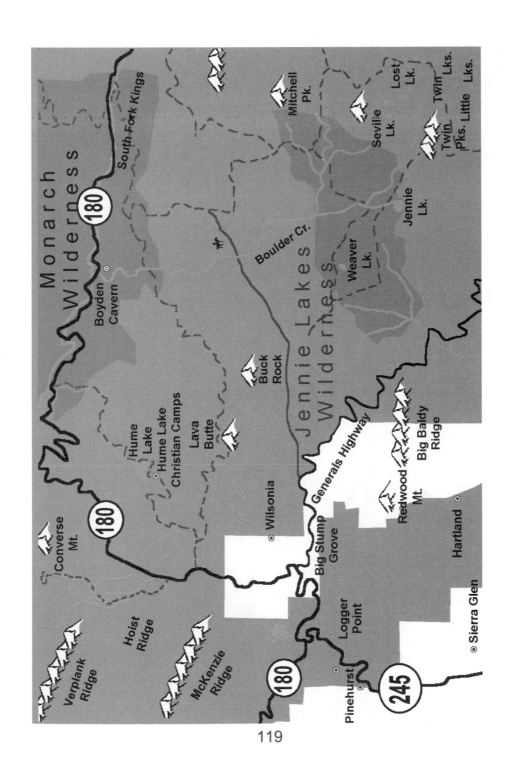

Jennie Lakes Wilderness

While not very widely known, this 10,971 acres of meadows, forests, lakes, and streams, features 26 miles of trails, including walking access to both Sequoia and Kings Canyon National Parks.

The Big Meadows area is a popular cross-country skiing and snow play destination. Jennie and Weaver lakes are favorites with fishermen. You can traverse 26 miles of trails within the Jennie Lakes Wilderness including the well used loop trail connecting the lakes. There is literally something for everyone to enjoy. Take along your camera, bring a picnic basket, plan to camp for a few days, the fishing is good. Perhaps you'll want to read a book under a shady tree.

The vegetation you'll encounter includes red fir, lodge pole pine, western white pine and an abundance of wildflowers in the spring. The lowest elevation is 7,000'. The highest is Mitchell Peak at 10,265'.

Jennie Lakes Wilderness is about 80 miles east of Fresno via State Highway 180 and the General's highway. There are four trail heads located on the Hume Lake Ranger District that access the Jennie Lakes Wilderness: Rowell Meadow (off road 13S14), Stony Creek (off Road 14S21), Marvin Pass (off Road 14S11). Hume Lake is 3 miles away and has a store with groceries, camping supplies, tackle and bait, lodging, a restaurant and fuel.

Horse Corral Pack Station
(559) 565-3404/564-6429
www.horsecorralpackers.com
Hume Lake Ranger District
(559) 338-2251

John Muir Wilderness

John Muir once said "… thousands of tired, nerve shaken, over-civilized people are beginning to find out that going to the mountains is going home; that wilderness is a necessity; that mountain parks and reservations are used not only as fountains of timber and irrigating rivers, but as fountains of life."

Since Muir uttered those words, millions of folks have taken them to heart and ventured forth in the forests that he so truly loved.

Countless trails now crisscross the beautiful Sierra Nevada, leading to many scenic visions of absolute splendor.

What could be more relaxing than sleeping out under the stars, listening to the sounds of the night?

There are 957 lakes and 627 miles of streams and rivers in the John Muir Wilderness. Awaiting your lure, bait or fly are Rainbow, brook, brown, golden and cutthroat trout. Any local sporting goods store can be sure you're outfitted properly for the particular part of the Wilderness to which you are headed.

Take care when hiking in the area. Many trails lead to high elevations which can literally take your breath away. Learn the symptoms of altitude sickness. Be careful, when hiking, of falling rocks. It's a good idea to stay away from steep cliff sides and obvious slide areas. Be prepared for any type of weather conditions. Mountain storms come quickly in any season, and they can include snow and icy conditions year round.

Make sure someone knows the route you are planning and when you are returning. Carry sufficient food, but don't take more weight than you can handle. Bears live throughout this area. Remember, you're the visitor! Use proper methods of storing food to avoid trouble with them. Don't feed them! If a bear approaches, bang pots and pans, yell, wave a coat. If the bear does not leave, you should. Report any such activities to the rangers. It's good to have a basic knowledge of backcountry first aid on the trail.

Horses and stock have the right-of-way on the trails. For the safety of all concerned, step off the trail and remain quiet until the animals have passed. Wilderness permits are required, a separate campfire permit is needed for use of campfires and stoves. Full details concerning the area and entry spots are noted for you at the right. Hunting is allowed, based upon the state game laws. Full details are to be found at the Ranger Stations. However, you cannot target shoot in any wilderness area at any time.

You'll also want to bring your camera along so you can take home some of the memories you'll have and share them.

The most important thing to remember is to travel safely and have a great time.

Eastern Entry

Fish Creek to Convict Lake
Mammoth Ranger District
(760) 924-5500

McGee Creek to Red Lake Trail
White Mountain Ranger District
(760) 873-2500

Taboose Pass to Horseshoe Meadow
Mt. Whitney Ranger District
(760) 876-5542

West Side Entry

Edison Lake to Florence Lake
and Crown Valley North
Pineridge Ranger District
(559) 841-3311

Florence Lake to Geraldine Lake
Dinkey Ranger Information Office
(559) 855-8321

Cedar Grove South
Wilderness Management Office
(559) 565-3306

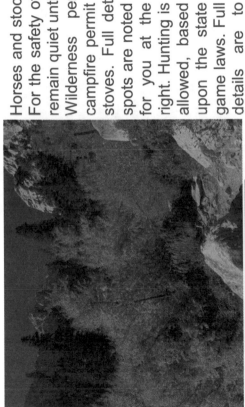

123

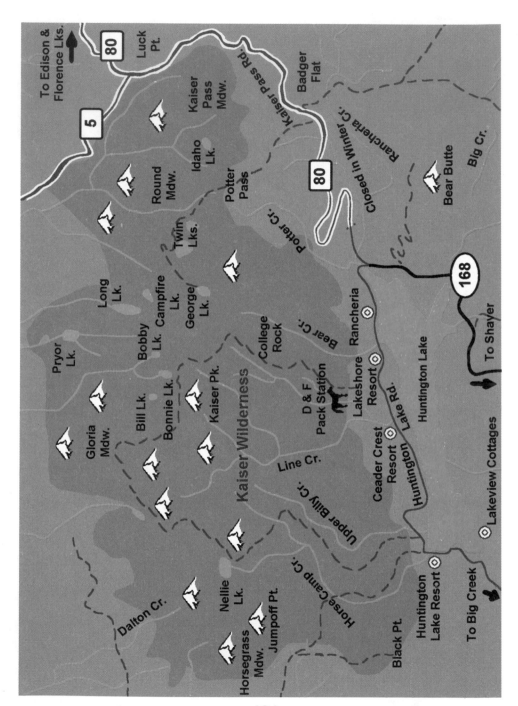

124

Kaiser Wilderness Area

Located north of Huntington Lake, 70 miles from Fresno, this was named after Kaiser Ridge, which divides the area into two different regions. Kaiser Peak, provides a commanding central Sierra Nevada view.

The southern portion rises gradually from the very popular Huntington Lake's north shore and has four trailheads. One trail leads to Coarsegrass Meadow, the next behind Upper Billy Creek camp area, takes you to Nellie Lake, Hidden Lake, and Gloria Meadow on the north side of Kaiser Ridge, and then on to the loop trail that traverses Kaiser Ridge to Kaiser Peak. Another way to this loop trail is from D&F Pack Station, behind Kinnikinnick campground. The Potter Pass Trail starts on Kaiser Pass Road near Badger Flat Campground. This and Potter Creek Trail provide access to the lakes in the northeast area of the Wilderness. The northern half is much more open. The descent from Kaiser Ridge into this area is very steep. Four trail-heads provide access into the area, the primary point of entry is from Sample Meadow Campground. Upper and Lower Twin Lakes and George Lake can be reached by trail. All other lakes are approached cross country. Winter storms start arriving in late October and snow generally remains on the ground until early June. A permit is required for all overnight stays. A quota system is in effect from the last Friday in June through mid September.

Pineridge Ranger District
(559) 855-5360
D&F Pack Station
(559) 893-3220
www.highsierrapackers.com

125

Kern County

Jedediah Smith led 17 men into the south end of the San Joaquin Valley in 1827, marking the first entry to the area by American explorers from the East. Gold was found in 1853, at rugged Greenhorn Gulch, just northwest of the upper Kern River. In 1860, Christian Bohna become the first permanent settler at Kern Island, the future site of Bakersfield. Col. Thomas Baker and his family arrived at Kern Island in 1863 and began turning swamp land into farming acreage.

By 1865, brothers Solomon and Philo Jewett had a large-scale cotton production at their Rio Bravo Ranch. Kern County was created in 1866, with Havilah as the county seat. A replica of the courthouse can be seen at the Havilah Courthouse Museum. Commercial oil production began in 1872. A hundred years later, the United Farm Worker's Union was born.

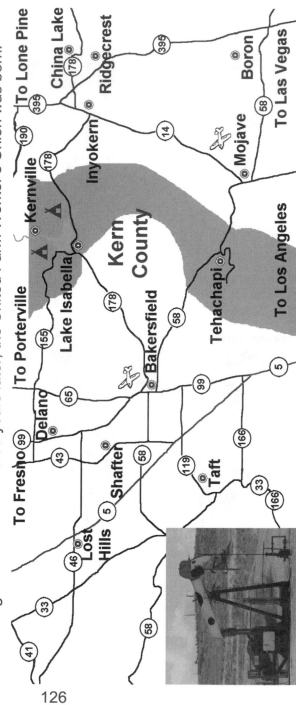

Places to visit - Ridgecrest is a favorite spot for rock collecting, panning for gold or touring the old mining community of Randsburg. Little Petroglyph Canyon, has American Indian drawings cut into the rocks. It is right in the midst of a Navy weapons development base at China Lake. Tours are offered through the Maturango Museum in Ridgecrest. The museum has a permanent display of the history of the Indian Wells Valley, the military and the mining interests. Silver City Ghost Town has 21 historic buildings with artifacts and mining displays.

Nestled at the foothills of the Sierra Nevada, Inyokern boasts a nice selection of antique stores, an observatory, an aviation museum and a brewery. It came alive in 1904 during the construction of the L.A. Aqueduct when it was known as Siding 16. Borate mining began in 1926 near Boron. Now U.S. Borax has the largest mine in California, producing borate ore around the clock from an open pit. Bootleggers in Boron built underground stills in the desert to brew whiskey for a thirsty L.A. Business was good until Prohibition ended in 1933. At Mojave, the Airport Civilian Flight Test Center has become home to cutting edge aviation technology in recent years.

Tehachapi, at 4,000', offers a break from the summer heat for folks who enjoy camping, fishing and hiking in the crisp mountain air. You will see huge windmills in the area, which create enough electricity to power San Francisco. You can also visit local ostrich farms.

Taft Airport is popular with skydivers, and the West Kern Oil Museum has old wooden oil derricks and photos of the Lakeview Gusher. Allensworth was established in 1908 as a self-governing and self-sustaining community for African Americans by Colonel Allensworth. It's now a State Park featuring restored structures.

Tule Elk State Reserve, 20 miles west of Bakersfield, off Stockdale Highway, is a 956-acre grassland reserve for one of the last remaining herds of rare tule elk.

127

Bakersfield County Chamber
(661) 327-4421
www.bakersfieldchamber.org
Colonel Allensworth Park
(661) 849-3433
Havilah Courthouse Museum
(661) 867-2643
www.ghosttowns.com
Maturango Museum
(760) 375-6900
www.ridgecrest.ca.us/~matmus
Silver City Ghost Town
(760) 379-5146
www.silvercityghosttown.cjb.net
Tule Elk State Reserve
(661) 764-6881
West Kern Oil Museum
(661) 765-6664

Kernville - Come Get Wet!

Nestled at the edge of the Kern River, this little town boasts lots of great water sport activities: fly fishing, white water rafting, swimming and nice accomodations! Kernville was founded in 1860 as Whiskey Flat on the land where Isabella Reservoir is now. The name was changed to Kernville in 1864 after prompting by ladies of a local church.

Kernville was moved in the early 1950s to make way for the construction of the Isabella Reservoir. The foundations of former homes are still visible today when the lake level is low. Dining and lodging is available overlooking the Kern River, with an array of cafes, shops and the Kern Valley Museum that features exhibits throughout the year showing a rich area history.

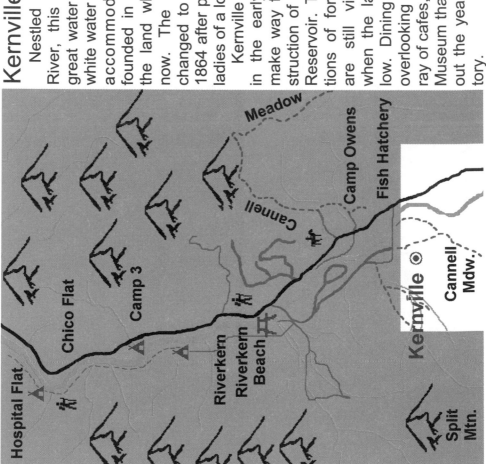

Meadow

Cannell

Camp Owens

Fish Hatchery

Chico Flat

Camp 3

Hospital Flat

Riverkern

Riverkern Beach

Kernville ◉

Cannell Mdw.

Split Mtn.

The Kern River Valley Art Association features work by area artists throughout the year. Just north of town, the Fish Hatchery gives visitors a close-up look at fish species found in the river and Isabella Reservoir.

Riverside Park is a favorite spot for lovely family picnics and strolls along the Kern River with that someone special. Circle Park in the heart of town features annual events including wildlife festivals, art shows and musical events.

Famed for whitewater rafting, Kernville is "the place" for river recreation. Outfitters on the Kern offer everything from one hour to three day rafting excursions. The town also is a hub for kayaking and mountain biking activities.

Not limited to water sports, many events are held in Kernville each year, including rodeos and a host of extreme sports. Rock climbing, hiking, fishing and camping also are enjoyed in the area.

Also popular is bird watching, with the spring Kern Valley Bioregions Festival and the fall Turkey Vulture Festival. Audubon California's Kern River Preserve in Weldon. Five bioregions in the area offer viewing many species during the year.

Kernville is also a gateway to the giant sequoias and the scenic wilderness of the Kern Plateau.

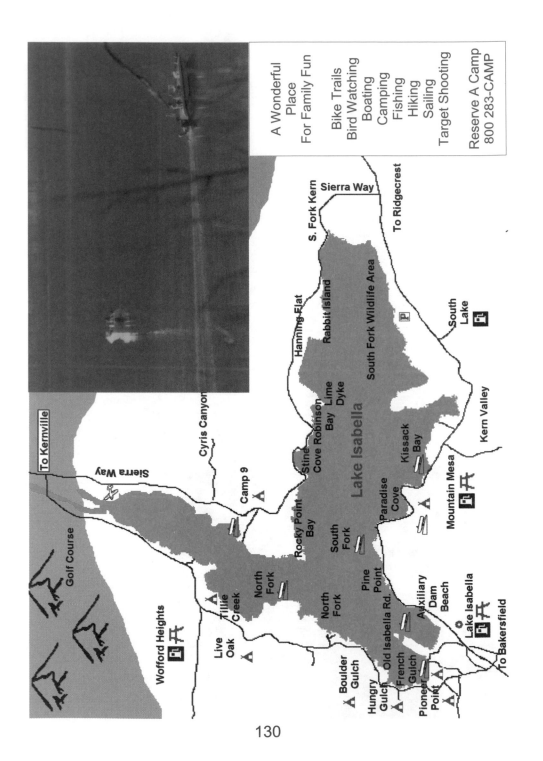

A Wonderful
Place
For Family Fun

Bike Trails
Bird Watching
Boating
Camping
Fishing
Hiking
Sailing
Target Shooting

Reserve A Camp
800 283-CAMP

Sierra Way

S. Fork Kern

To Ridgecrest

Hanning Flat

Rabbit Island

South Fork Wildlife Area

South Lake

Cyris Canyon

Sierra Way

To Kernville

Camp 9

Stine Cove

Robinson Bay

Lime Dyke

Lake Isabella

Kern Valley

Rocky Point Bay

South Fork

Paradise Cove

Kissack Bay

Mountain Mesa

Golf Course

Wofford Heights

Tillie Creek

North Fork

North Fork

Pine Point

Auxiliary Dam Beach

Lake Isabella

To Bakersfield

Live Oak

Boulder Gulch

Hungry Gulch

French Gulch

Old Isabella Rd.

Pioneer Point

130

The town is predominantly residential with a large population of retired residents. Lake Isabella has retained a rural atmosphere with strong roots to the area's ranching history. Cattle can often been seen grazing between the main boulevard and the freeway. With its two stop lights, Lake Isabella is the business and service hub of the Kern River Valley.

It supplies the surrounding mountain folks, campers and those just traveling through with grocery stores, full service gas stations, drug stores, fast food establishments, banks, restaurants, medical facilities and retail stores. The friendly, small town atmosphere is evident annually during the Lake Isabella Christmas Parade.

One of the largest reservoirs in the California's southern end with 11,000 surface acres, it offers year round water sports to keep the visitors coming to enjoy such activities as boating, fishing, water skiing, sailing, target shooting, hiking and off-road vehicle trails. Several campgrounds operated by the Sequoia National Forest surround the lake. Auxiliary Dam and Paradise Cove campgrounds are located at the south end of the lake off Highway 178.

The Main Dam campground offers 82 campsites off Highway 155. Pioneer Point, French Gulch (groups of 100 or more), Boulder Gulch and Hungry Gulch are all located on the west side of the lake off Highway 155. Tillie Creek, Live Oak South and Live Oak North campgrounds are off Highway 155 south of Wofford Heights.

On the east side of the lake there is the private Camp 9 campground and Stine Cove Recreation Area. Some of the above campgrounds are developed campgrounds, for which reservations are recommended on holidays. Bring a hat and sunscreen.

For Reservations
(877) 444-6777
U.S. Forest Service
(760) 379-5646
Basic Area Information
(760) 379-5646
www.kernvalley.com

Upper Kern Canyon
Hiking Trails

Many exciting trails are available to explore on the Canneil Meadow Ranger District.

They include:

Whiskey Flat - 14.5	Rincon - 19.5
Cannell - 12	
Packsaddle - 2.3	Flynn Canyon - 3.9
Tobias - 4.6	River Trail - 5.2

Watch for snakes during the spring and summer. Pets are permitted on the trails.

Be careful of fire. Carry water with you. Visitors should not drink directly from the creeks, springs or river. Recommended treatment is to bring the water to a rolling boil for five minutes or use a filter purification system.

Kernville Ranger Station
(760) 376-3781

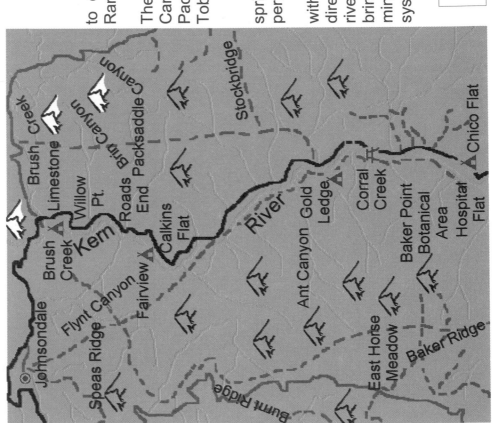

The Upper Kern River area is known for it's spring runoff and action packed white water rafting trips, but it's also a wonderful place for mountain biking and rock climbing on the steep bluffs that line the river and in the surrounding mountains. There are excellent trails for hikers and those who enjoy horseback riding.

Several campgrounds are located along the river's banks and open camping is permitted almost everywhere along the stream and in

the mountains as long as you have a valid campfire permit.

Whitewater rafting runs for beginners and experts are located along the river from above Kernville to below Lake Isabella in the Kern River Canyon. You'll want to have your camera with you, and keep your eyes open for wildlife in the canyon. You'll also want to know what poison oak and poison ivy are, and make sure that you avoid them.

You'll find the Audubon's Kern River Preserve, along the banks of the river's South Fork near highway 178. It's popular with nature lovers for the tours along its trails.

Audubon's River Preserve
(760) 378-2531
Cannell Meadow Ranger
(760) 376-3781
Campground Reservations
(877) 444-6777
www.reserveusa.com
Kernville Chamber
(760) 376-2629

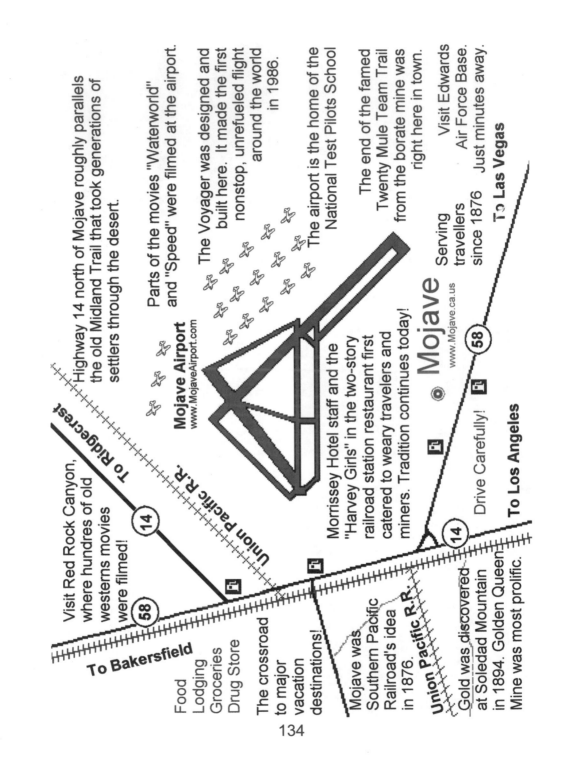

Highway 14 north of Mojave roughly parallels the old Midland Trail that took generations of settlers through the desert.

Parts of the movies "Waterworld" and "Speed" were filmed at the airport.

The Voyager was designed and built here. It made the first nonstop, unrefueled flight around the world in 1986.

The airport is the home of the National Test Pilots School

The end of the famed Twenty Mule Team Trail from the borate mine was right here in town.

Visit Edwards Air Force Base. Just minutes away.

To Las Vegas

Mojave Airport
www.MojaveAirport.com

Visit Red Rock Canyon, where hundres of old westerns movies were filmed!

To Ridgecrest

Union Pacific R.R.

Morrissey Hotel staff and the "Harvey Girls" in the two-story railroad station restaurant first catered to weary travelers and miners. Tradition continues today!

Mojave
www.Mojave.ca.us

Serving travellers since 1876

Drive Carefully!

58

14

To Los Angeles

Food
Lodging
Groceries
Drug Store

The crossroad to major vacation destinations!

To Bakersfield

58

Mojave was Southern Pacific Railroad's idea in 1876.

Union Pacific R.R.

Gold was discovered at Soledad Mountain in 1894. Golden Queen Mine was most prolific.

14

134

Kings Canyon Park

Famous for it's deep canyons, rushing water, giant Sequoias and beautiful panoramic views, the park also has scenic backcountry trails, an abundance of photogenic wildlife and an opportunity to explore caves.

Enjoy the varied outdoor activities like camping, fishing, horseback riding, hiking, white water rafting, cross country skiing and seeing some of the tallest trees in the world.

A variety of lodging facilities is available in the park and the nearby communities just outside this marvel of nature! Several campgrounds and backcountry camp sites await you.

Grant Grove has pay showers and a laundry, which are available year-round with limited hours.

Keep in mind that no motor vehicle fuel is sold in the park. Make sure you have a full tank when you enter.

Most vacation supplies are offered by the various facilities in the park.

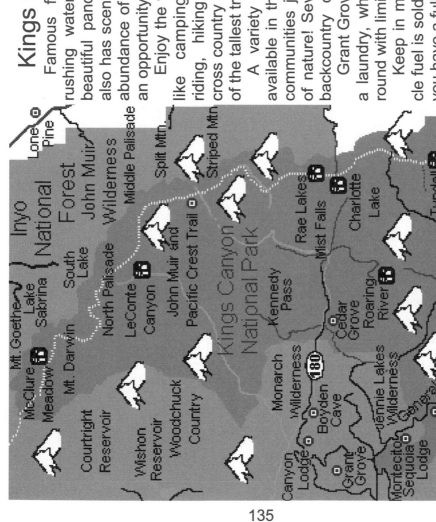

Boyden Cavern

This cave is found at the bottom of the deepest canyon in the U.S., the spectacular 8,000' deep Kings River Canyon.

It lies beneath the massive 2,000' high marble walls of the famous Kings Gates. This magnificent cavern has many varieties of natural speleothems, including rare "shield" formations. Visitors are delighted to find the spectacular beauty above ground is complimented by this natural beauty underground. A 45-minute tour, suitable for kids to senior citizens, begins with a steep 5-minute walk to the cavern entrance. From there you travel deep within, where the temperature is a constant 55F. Groups follow a well-lighted and hand-rail equipped trail as guides point out many natural varieties of formations. Tours leave approximately every hour on the hour. For safety reasons, children are not allowed to be carried in backpacks on this

April, May and October
11 a.m. - 4 p.m. every day
June to September
10 a.m. - 5 p.m. every day
(866) 762-2837
www.caverntours.com

Cedar Grove

On your way along Highway 180 into Cedar Grove, you'll see a variety of vegetation. Entering Kings Canyon National Park, you'll be in rich, forested lands. As you reach the rim of the deep canyon, where you'll see the forks of the Kings River uniting, it's almost like being in a high desert area.

After you pass over the bridge near Boyden Caverns, you start back into the forest. Make plans to stop at Grizzley Falls, especially in late spring and early summer. The runoff mist will cool you down and the view is spectacular. There are picnic facilities, so why not have lunch.

More beautiful waterfalls, several scenic hiking trails that feature panoramic views, plus fishing, camping and more await you as you come into this wonderful area!

Cedar Grove Village includes camping, lodging, restaurant, a Visitor's Center and the Road's End Wilderness Permit Station. For your convenience there is also a market and gift shop, a coin operated laundry and showers.

This is bear territory, so use your bear-proof food containers for safety. If you are venturing into the back country, either get a portable bear-proof container or use proper food hanging techniques to avoid encounters with bears. Remember, you're the visitor!

Sequoia-Kings Canyon Services
(559) 335-5505
www.sequoia-kingscanyon.com
Cedar Grove Pack Station
(559) 565-3464 or 564-3231
National Park Service
www.nps.gov/seki/cgf&s.htm.

138

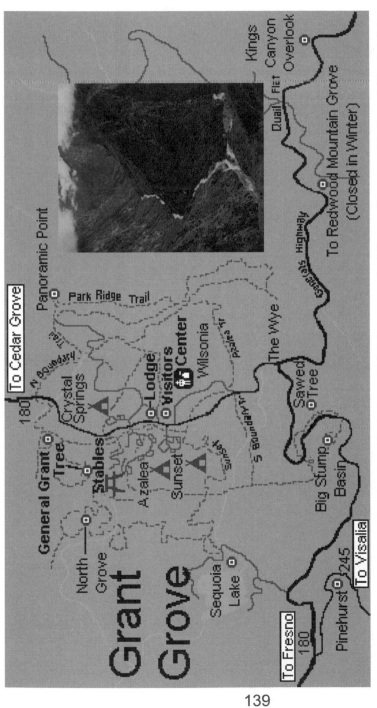

Grant Grove is close to the Highway 180 Entrance to Kings Canyon National Park. It is home to the General Grant Tree, known as the "Nation's Christmas Tree". It is the country's only living shrine, dedicated to commemorating those Americans who lost their lives in war. The area around Grant Grove is alive "historically", with many interesting places to visit. You can stay at the John Muir Lodge or choose other lodging facilities or a nice campground.

Services offered include a grocery store, restaurant, gift shop, horseback riding, a laundry and shower facilities, a U.S. Post Office and seasonal snow play rentals.

One of the trails you can trek is Panoramic Point, a 1/4 mile walk that takes you to a spectacular view of the Sierra Nevada. You can see Eagle Scout Peak in Sequoia Park and Mt. Goddard in Kings Canyon Park. Redwood Canyon is among the larger sequoia groves, and contains Hart Tree, one of the 20 largest sequoias. The trailhead is two miles down a "challenging" road five miles south of Grant Grove.

Big Stump Basin is where you'll find the remains of Smith Comstock's lumber operations. This is a mile loop walk through regenerating sequoia forest trees. There are lots of birds and wildflowers to see too!

Sequoia Lake Overlook is a two mile hike, taking you through the Dead Giant Loop, where you'll see a huge dead sequoia that shows axe marks girdling the tree. You'll also see a historic mill pond and beautiful scenery.

North Grove is found after a lovely walk through meadows and along creeks, seeing mixed conifers and the sequoia forest. It is a mile and a half stroll that starts at the Grant Tree parking lot.

Grant Grove Stables is near the Village. Come enjoy a 1 or 2 hour ride. Open all summer from 8 a.m. to 6 p.m.

Sequoia-Kings Canyon Services
(559) 335-5505
Grant Grove Pack Station
(559) 335-9292 or 564-3231
National Park Service
www.nps.gov/seki/cgf&s.htm.

Breathtaking views offering many nice photographic shots are quite common in Kings Canyon and Sequoia National Parks. Each day brings different colors out of the Sierra. Be sure to bring lots of film!

A fantastic place for a family style vacation, literally something for everyone to enjoy! Open all year!

Madera County

Many settlers in the early 1850s had their eyes on gold, but soon found most miners earned $1 a day.

Most switched to other enterprises. They found the land was rich and the water plentiful. Thus farming and the cattle ranching industry became very prosperous.

Wine grapes, raisin grapes and wheat are some of the crops harvested by early farmers.

Mines and towns needed timber, so others turned to logging. A unique method to send timber to the Valley was created: a V-shaped, water filled flume. Occasionally, loggers used special boats to get down the flume at speeds reportedly up to 80 miles per hour!

To North Fork →

Coarsegold

Fine Gold

200

O'Neals

200

211

Millerton

Friant

206

San Joaquin River Parkway

To Clovis

To Oakhurst

Texas Mine

Raymond Road

41

Enterprise

Grub Gulch

415

Knowles

Granite Quarry

400

Madera County

411

Hensley Lake

41

Four Corners

Valley Children's Hospital

41

To Fresno

To Mariposa

600

Bossert Ranch

Eastman Lake

Raymond

607

603

600

Highway 145

400

Buchanan

607

28 1/2 Rd.

607

Madera

99

To Fresno

To Merced

142

Madera, which is the word for lumber in Spanish, was formed in 1875, as the timber started arriving at the railhead via the flume.

This area was originally part of Fresno County. In 1893, it was designated Madera County by the legislature. Mining, ranching and farming are still important to this area, along with light industry and tourism. You can watch bald eagles fly while you fish or go boating on Bass Lake. You can still pan for gold and see many old buildings and historical places. Great lodging and camping facilities are available. A number of restaurants, both fast food and those offering elegant dining experiences, are scattered throughout the area. Enjoy hiking, fishing, boating, horseback riding and exploring the back country.

Eastern Madera Chamber
(559) 683-7766
www.sierratel.com/chamber

143

Bass Lake

This is the home of many popular family retreats, resorts, spots to fish, camping sites and trails on which to hike, mountain bike or ride horses. In the winter, you can cross country ski, ride snowmobiles or just enjoy building snow men with the kids.

The Pines Resort is a full service facility for families or a wonderful place to take someone very special.

You can take a tour of the lake, and during part of the year, see eagles nesting here.

The Pines Resort
(559) 642-3121
(800) 350-7463
www.basslake.com

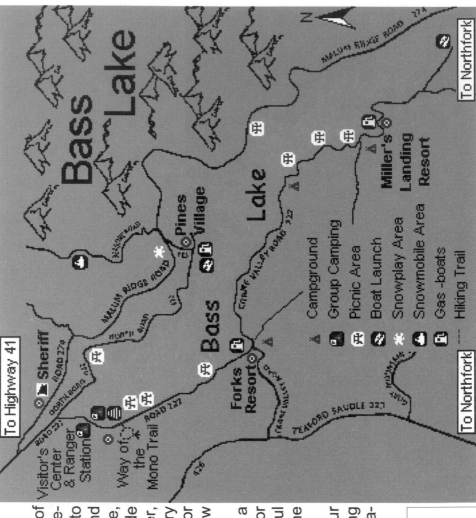

144

Fuel is available, along with repairs, snacks and cool drinks. In Pines Village, you see a movie or browse the antique shops and local art galleries. There's also a U.S. Post Office and a general store.

The lake is stocked with trout, bass, salmon, catfish, crappie and bluegill. Most folks like to fish from a boat, but good catches are made from along the shoreline too.

Water skiing, wind surfing and jet skiing are excellent and visitors appreciate that the water is warm, 75 to 78 degrees in the summer.

If you come to the area around the Fourth of July, join thousands of others for a whole day of activities, capped off with a giant fireworks display.

Rock climbers find many challenges around the area. Big walls, like El Capitan in nearby Yosemite, can take a week to ascend. Many spectacular back country crags are in the Sierra Nevada surrounding the lake.

Ride your mountain bike on trails that range from easy to challenging. There's a vast network of trails, fire roads and old railroad grades in the area. You can ride for hours without ever encountering anyone else!

145

You'll want to drop by The Forks Resort, home of the famous "Forks Burger". It is across the lake and like Miller's Landing, up the road apiece, has everything you need to help make your visit a great experience.

Cabins, great food, a marina with rentals and fuel await you at both well staffed on-the-water facilities, along with fishing licenses, tackle and bait.

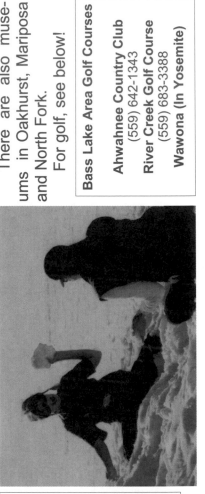

Hiking trails include the Willow Creek Trail passes along Angel Falls. Be careful, there are hazardous sections on the trail. During the spring, cascades of water flow into deep pools. The Way of the Mono Trail is a half mile self guided walking trail detailing the lives of the Western Mono Indians. You'll see authentic grinding holes and pretty views of the lake.

Goat Mountain Trail is a strenuous hike, climbing four miles to a mountain summit where a fire lookout tower provides grand views of the Sierra Nevada and Bass Lake.

There are also museums in Oakhurst, Mariposa and North Fork.

For golf, see below!

Coarsegold

Don't miss the annual rodeo! Year round there's good food and lodging, plus supplies, a gold panning facility, a museum and other attractions that entice visitors to this tiny Madera County town.

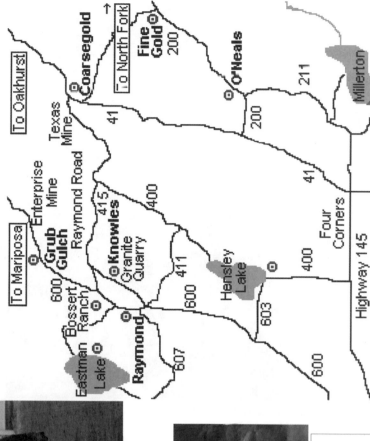

To Oakhurst

To North Fork ↑

To Mariposa

Coarsegold

Fine Gold

O'Neals

Millerton

Enterprise Mine

Texas Mine

Grub Gulch

Raymond Road

Knowles

Granite Quarry

Hensley Lake

Four Corners

Highway 145

Bossert Ranch

Eastman Lake

Raymond

41

200

211

200

415

400

41

411

600

603

600

600

607

Eastman Lake

Built in 1976, the lake is used for flood control, irrigation, recreation and wildlife management. It's less than an hour's drive from Madera. It sits among tall grasses and scattered oak trees.

Camping is available year round. There are group camp facilities and an equestrian staging area.

Fishing is popular, with bass, crappie, bluegill, catfish and rainbow trout vying for your bait. There are two launching areas for boats. No matter if you have a sailboat, jet ski, row boat or power boat, this is a fun place to spend some time.

Hunting for rabbits, squirrels, dove, quail and waterfowl is allowed during the relevant seasons. With a special park permit, archery hunters can also try for deer. Always be extremely careful when hunting.

Camping Reservations
(877) 444-6777
www.reserveusa.com
Group Camping Information
(559) 689-3255

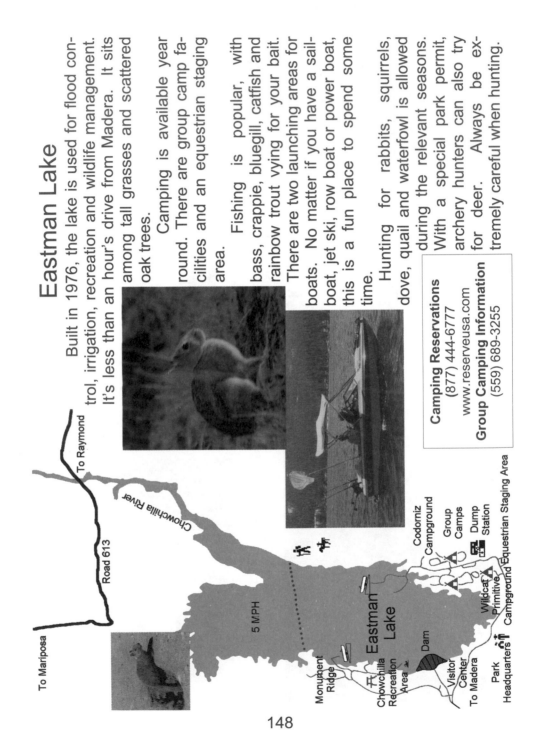

148

Hensley Lake

The weekly fishing reports from Hensley Lake tell of good to excellent bass fishing year round. Not far from the old mining site of Raymond, the lake is situated in the Madera foothills.

You'll travel through ranch land dotted with cows and also populated by a variety of interesting birds, large and small. There are picnic spots for day use and camping facilities for those staying awhile! There's a beach for swimming, plus trails for hiking and horseback riding enthusiasts.

Camping Reservations
(877) 444-6777
www.reserveusa.com

To Raymond

Road 407

Wildlife Area

5 MPH

Wildlife Area

Buck Ridge Day-Use Area

5 MPH

HiddenView Campground

5 MPH

Park Headquarters

Hensley Lake

5 MPH

Road 603

Road 400

149

Mammoth Pools

The road to this area is called the Sierra Vista Scenic Byway. As you wander along its 100 miles of panoramic scenes, you can stop to fish, hike, camp or have a picnic. You'll find some secluded camp-sites right along high country streams.

Drive up to the Nelder Grove, where Bull Buck, one of the oldest and largest giant sequoias, is located. Take a half-mile hike up to Fresno Dome, with its glaciation effects and spectacular view. Bring a camera!

Minarets Ranger Station
(559) 877-2218

Granite Creek
Clover
Meadow
Minarets
Pack Station
Arch Rock
Bowler
Jackass Rock
Upper Chiquito
Soquel Meadow
Grays Mountain
Jones Store
Fresno Dome
Kelty Meadow
Nelder Grove
Texas Flat
Redwood
Lower Chiquito
Little Jackass
China Bar Boat Camp
Wagner's Store
Mammoth Pools
Placer
Soda Springs
Sweetwater
Windy Point
Mile High Vista

Scenic Byway

To Bass Lake

To North Fork

150

Wagner's Store

The Wagner family has served visitors to the area for many years. Located conveniently across the creek from the campgrounds, you'll find a mixture of warm hospitality and a fully stocked mountain store.

They also sell fuel and oil for boats and motor vehicles. Be aware this is only place in the Mammoth Pools area that you can purchase vehicle fuel. Picnic tables are right outside the front door, so you can have a snack and rest awhile.

If you're a horseman, you're welcome to bring your animals into the area, where the Wagners will let you corral them for awhile. You'll need to bring feed, since there is not enough vegetation to adequately feed your livestock.

The staff will gladly point you toward the launching facility at Mammoth Pools. Lots of hungry Rainbow trout need you to drop them a worm or two, along with some Power Bait for dessert. Keep in mind that use of the lake is restricted from May 1 to June 15 due to deer migration. However, area campgrounds remain open and there is good fishing along the river. It's quite refreshing to take a swim in the lake. However, the water is from backcountry runoff and can be very cold! There are a number of trails for hikers and horseback riders in the surrounding forests.

Wagners Store
Memorial Day Weekend to Oct. 1
(559) 841-3736

Minarets Pack Station

Located on the Sierra Vista Scenic Byway at Miller Meadow, near the junction of Minarets and Beasore Roads, the folks at the Minarets Pack Station offer day rides and backcountry pack trips. They serve Ansel Adams Wilderness and southeastern Yosemite National Park, with their season running from June through October.

No matter if you enjoy fishing, photography, hiking, hunting or family fun, nothing can quite compare to the scenic panorama of the Western Sierra. Banner Peak and Mount Ritter are towering peaks. The exciting white water of the middle fork of the San Joaquin River and all the quiet and peaceful lakes and streams in between offer great fishing and lifelong memories. There are several options for you.

Take a spot trip. You furnish camping gear and supplies and they put you and the gear on friendly livestock and take you to a suitable campsite. The packer unloads the stock and takes them back to the pack station. They'll return for you on a prearranged date. From your campsite you can hike to other lakes, streams and mountain peaks. They have a Deluxe Trip where they provide everything you need, except clothing and sleeping bag. They send along a packer, cook and stock for the duration of your trip. You just relax and enjoy yourself on this trip. Call for details!

Minarets Pack Station
(559) 868-3405
www.highsierrpackers.org/min.htm

152

North Fork
Exact Center of California!

Not far from the center of North Fork is the Exact Center of the State of California. That's what the town folks say. Hey, they've got facts and measurements and paperwork to back up the statement.

Like most of the communities in the Sierra foothills, settlers first came around searching for gold. But, here timber was to be the key to a thriving town. The mill was shut down in the 1980s much to the dismay of the locals. There are many activities that vacationers will find interesting. The Sierra Mono Indian Museum features artifacts from the local Mono tribe. Bass Lake, Mammoth Pools and the San Joaquin River offer fishing, hiking and boating.

You can find ample lodging, including several Bed & Breakfast establishments at which you can stay during your visit. The town has several good places to eat, service stations, grocery stores and other services you may need.

The climate and elevation support a wide variety of plant and animal life, including mule deer, black bear, squirrels, chipmunks, bobcat, coyotes, gray fox, beaver, rabbit, pikas, porcupine, marmot and mountain quail. There are also 31 species of fish. In the spring, wildflowers paint the hillsides.

North Fork Chamber
(559) 877-4477
www.north-fork-chamber.com
Sierra Mono Indian Museum
(559) 877-2115

Historic Oakhurst

Once known as Fresno Flats in the 1850s, the town supplied mines, miners, lumber companies and loggers with necessary provisions at the southern end of the old "Highway 49".

Today, you can visit Fresno Flat Historical Park, where a number of historical buildings have been preserved. Tours are very interesting and educational.

Now an important gateway to Yosemite and the Sierra Nevada in general, the community now supplies vacationers as they explore the local area or venture further up the highway. You'll find everything you need to make your vacation a success.

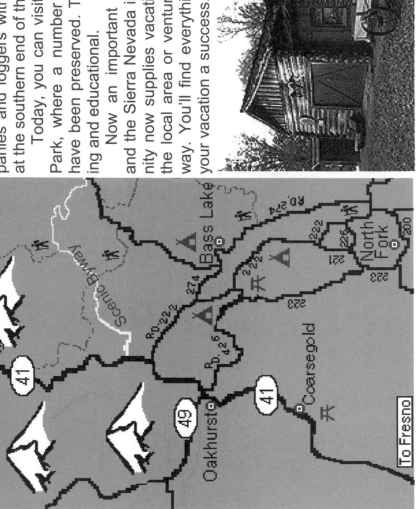

Aside from the many art galleries and antique shops you can browse, you'll want to see the old fashioned show at the Golden Chain Theatre. See what happens to little ole "Nell".

When it's time to settle down for the evening, your choices for lodging are varied. There are full service hotels, motels and Bed & Breakfast inns.

Dining is another experience all together. You can choose from your favorite fast food joint or elegant restaurants. You might enjoy an early morning stop at one of the famous bakeries along Highway 41.

While in the area, you should stop by the Yosemite Sierra Visitors Bureau for a rundown on exactly what you might be able to do in and around the community. They have all the information you need to help make your visit an experience that you'll treasure forever.

155

Yosemite Sierra Visitor's Bureau
(559) 876-1234
www.go2yosemite.com
Golden Chain Theatre
(559) 683-7112
Eastern Madera County Chamber
(559) 683-7766
Campground Information
(559) 642-3212
Fresno Flats Historical Museum
(559) 683-6570

Mariposa County

Home to California's oldest seat of justice still in use, the original building was completed in 1854.

An English-made clock, that featured a 267 lb. bell in the cupola, was installed in 1860. It has been faithfully tolling each hour ever since.

The courtroom, scene of many famous legal battles, civil and criminal, remains the same as in pioneer days, with the original seats, tables, and judge's bench.

Mariposa is "the Mother" of many California counties. Eleven in fact, were formed from the original 1850 Mariposa County: Merced, Madera, Fresno, Kings, Tulare, Kern, much of Mono and Inyo, and parts of San Benito, Los Angeles and San Bernadino.

Enjoy the varied and rich history of Mariposa and other towns along the famous old Gold Rush Trail, known today as Highway 49.

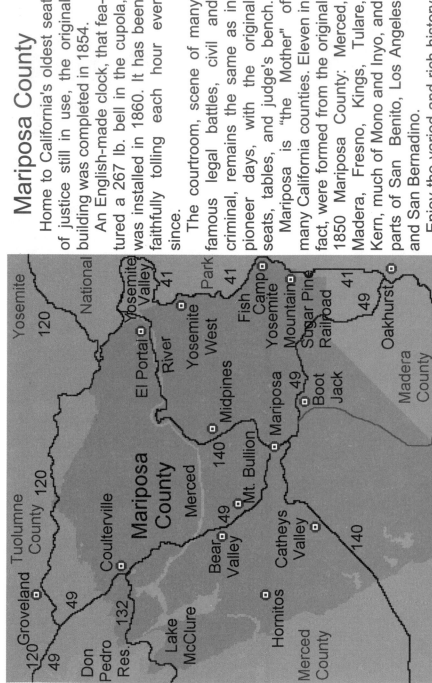

While here, you can visit colorful towns like Greeley Hill, Cathey's Valley, Boot Jack, Fish Camp, El Portal, Midpines, and the more historical communities of Coulterville, Hornitos, Mount Bullion, and Bear Valley.

Remnants of early mining settlements still retain their interesting old names such as Dogtown, Briceburg, Mormon Bar, Bridgeport and Bagby. Speaking of names, "Mariposa" is the Spanish term for butterfly.

Tour the California State Mining and Mineral Museum where you can see the Fricot Nugget, a magnificent piece of crystallized gold from El Dorado County. It weighs 201.40 troy ounces and is one of the finest and largest specimens of native gold in existence. You'll also want tc explore the Mariposa County Museum and Historical Center.

You can stay in bed and breakfast establishments, campgrounds, motels and hotels. The food is great. There are museums to visit, fish to catch, rivers to raft, horses to ride and lots of things to record on film. The many back country roads give you a feel of what it was like during the early years in the area.

Mariposa Chamber
(209) 966-2456
www.mariposa.org
California State Mining and Mineral Museum
(209) 742-7625
Mariposa County Museum and History Center
(209) 966-2924

157

Bear Valley

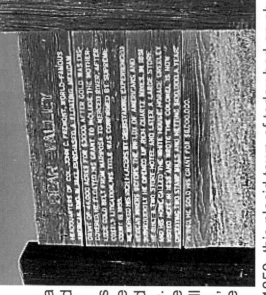

First called Johnsonville, Bear Valley had a population of 3,000 including Chinese, Cornish, and Mexicans, all looking for gold.

During 1850-60 when Col. John C. Fremont's Pine Tree and Josephine mines were producing, he built an elegant hotel, the Oso House. It was created with lumber brought around the Horn by ship.

Unfortunately, it no longer stands, due to a fire in 1888. Many structures were rebuilt. Those still standing include: Bon Ton Saloon, Trabucco Store, Odd Fellows Hall, school house and remains of the jail, all reminders of Bear Valley's colorful past.

The nearby old town of Hornitos was settled in 1850, this placid town of today had an obstreperous reputation in the mid-1800's. The notorious bandit, Joaquin Murietta, was known to be a frequent visitor. Tour the area and see the ruins of several old buildings, like the old jail and Domingo Ghiradelli's store. He became famous as the "chocolate king". Built before 1869, St. Catherine's Catholic Church and cemetery sit atop a hill overlooking the town.

No matter where you are in Recreational Rich Mariposa County there is always something close at hand to enjoy. These activities include: hiking, mountain biking, camping, gold panning, swimming, nature trails, tennis, golf, boating, hang gliding, skiing, rafting, fishing, and exploring.
Browse the many antique shops in the small towns as you visit!

Coulterville

While the miners worked the nearby streams and the foothills for veins of gold, the gamblers, outlaws and fancy ladies worked the miners for the same prize. Meanwhile, George W. Coulter moved in to serve their needs with a general store and hotel. His first store was established in 1850, which consisted of a tent stocked with merchandise hauled into the foothills by pack train.

The settlement was, at first, called Banerita, from the flag flying over Coulter's store. A post office established in 1853 was called Maxwell Creek, but changed the next year to honor Coulter. Coulter and the town which took his name prospered, as Coulterville became the business and social capital of the area.

The hundreds of miners working the rich placers of Maxwell, Boneyard, and Black Creeks helped him become firmly established. He built the first hotel. Water for it was pumped from a well by two Newfoundland dogs. The first stamp mill for crushing quartz ore was built here by Andrew Goss. The nearby quartz mines, using very crude methods, with only wood for fuel, operated for years producing millions. The community has been designed as State Historical Landmark No. 332. Few changes have been made to it since the turn of the century.

Here you'll find the Northern Mariposa County History Center, an outstanding gold rush history museum. You can stay at the Hotel Jeffery and relax at the Magnolia Saloon. Both have been family owned and operated since 1851.

159

Fish Camp

Just outside the western entrance to Yosemite National Park, this is a mountain resort featuring a variety of activities.

Tenaya Lodge offers a full service hotel and conference center facility with several extra recreational programs available for the guests. Both the Apple Tree and the Narrow Gauge Inns have accommodations for couples and families.

For those enjoying a Bed & Breakfast environment, the area has several from which to choose. There are also camping sites nearby, as well as a general store and a Post Office.

The Yosemite Trails Pack Station has a number of horseback riding programs for visitors. In addition to providing one and two hour rides, they can plan an exciting back country pack trip for you. During the summer evenings, they also offer a Chuck-wagon Jamboree in conjunction with the Tenaya Lodge. Enjoy an evening wagon ride, a fantastic all you can eat barbeque feast and singing around the campfire.

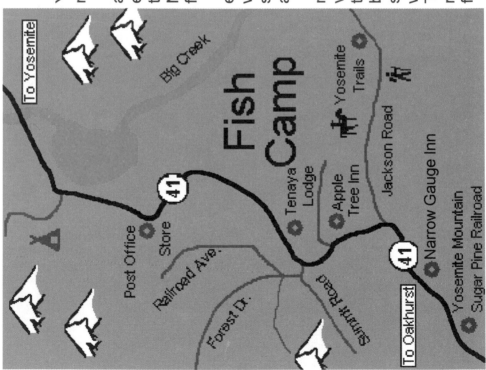

On weekends and holidays in the winter time, you can take a sleigh ride, or ride horses in the snow. Make arrangements through Tenaya Lodge.

Speaking of winter, Badger Pass Ski Area is a great family attraction. It's geared for all levels and specializes in teaching folks to ski. There are also good cross country skiing trails.

Jackson Road is also a favorite of snowmobile riders, snowshoe enthusiasts and those just interested in snow play.

Golf is nearby at Wawona, just eight miles up the road. The Mariposa Grove of sugar pines and giant sequoias is only six miles.

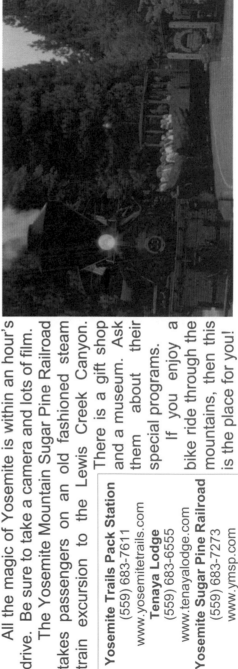

All the magic of Yosemite is within an hour's drive. Be sure to take a camera and lots of film.

The Yosemite Mountain Sugar Pine Railroad takes passengers on an old fashioned steam train excursion to the Lewis Creek Canyon. There is a gift shop and a museum. Ask them about their special programs.

If you enjoy a bike ride through the mountains, then this is the place for you!

Yosemite Trails Pack Station
(559) 683-7611
www.yosemitetrails.com
Tenaya Lodge
(559) 683-6555
www.tenayalodge.com
Yosemite Sugar Pine Railroad
(559) 683-7273
www.ymsp.com

Mariposa - The County Seat, Since 1850

This mortise and tenon Greek Revival courthouse, erected in 1854, is California's oldest court of law and has served continuously as the seat of government since 1854. During the 19th century, landmark mining cases, setting legal precedent, were tried here. Much United States mining law is based on decisions emanating from this historic courthouse.

Other historic buildings still standing include the 1863 St. Joseph's Catholic Church, the 1859 jail, the 1866 Trabucco Warehouse and the 1866 Schlageter Hotel.

Visit the Mariposa Museum & History Center. It presents an authentic picture of people and life in Mariposa County from the Indian and Spanish periods to the famed Gold Rush era up to the recent past.

See original documents, artifacts and artwork, as well as a typical one-room miner's cabin and displays of the life style of the West's most famous explorer and Mariposa County resident, John C. Fremont, and his wife, Jessie. Outdoor exhibits include mining equipment and an Indian village.

The California Mining and Mineral Museum is just three miles from Mariposa. See displays of the State's historic gem and mineral collection, with over 20,000 unique specimens. Plan to spend the afternoon.

The display appeals to the curiosity and fascination of mineral collectors and is one of the largest in the world.

Many of the gems and minerals in the collection were discovered during the mid and late 1800's; donated to the state for safekeeping and for the enjoyment and education of the public.

Yosemite, one of the most magnificent of the national parks is right in the town's backyard.

It is characterized by waterfalls and glacier-eroded landscapes. You can make Mariposa a base camp for day trips to many great destinations. Enjoy horseback rides, hiking and mountain bike trails, rock climbing, golf and fishing. In the winter there's skiing, both alpine and cross country, snowmobile trails and snow play. There are campsites and houseboat rentals. It's open year round.

Lake McClure has boating, fishing and swimming. There are campsites and houseboat rentals. It's open year round.

Mariposa has lodging and dining facilities for every taste. Vacation supplies, vehicle service and medical services are readily available.

Lake McClure Recreational Area
(800) 468-8889
Yosemite National Park
(209) 372-0265

Merced River

The ideal river for adventurous beginners or the more seasoned rafters, the Merced tumbles over Yosemite's Vernal Falls, meandering through the valley, building into a frenzy of pure whitewater fun. It is characterized by a steep gradient, sweeping bends, and few obstacles to hinder a raft's momentum. It moves through a grassy mid-Sierra canyon dotted with oak and digger pine. Those on early spring trips are treated to wondrous hillsides decorated in golden poppies, purple lupine, and wild iris. For the biggest waves and longest rapids one should plan a trip during April or May, usually the months of peak runoff. See the mist from the impressive North Fork Falls, a 30' unrunnable waterfall which you portage. Camping and lodging are available along with several outfitters that will help plan a trip!

Ahwahnee Whitewater
(800) 359-9790
www.ahwahnee.com
American River Recreation
(800) 333-7238
www.arrafting.com
O.A.R.S. Inc.
(800) 346-6277
www.oars.com
White Water Excitement
(800) 750-2386
www.wwenic.com
Whitewater Voyages
(800) 400-7238
www.whitewatervoyages.com

All Outdoors Inc.
(800) 274-2387
www.aorafting.com
Mariah Adventure Connection
(800) 556-6060
www.raftcalifornia.com
Zephyr Whitewater Expeditions
(800) 431-3636
www.zrafting.com
Yosemite Trails Camp
(209) 966-6444
www.yosemitetrailcamp.com
Arta
(800) 323-2782
www.arta.org

164

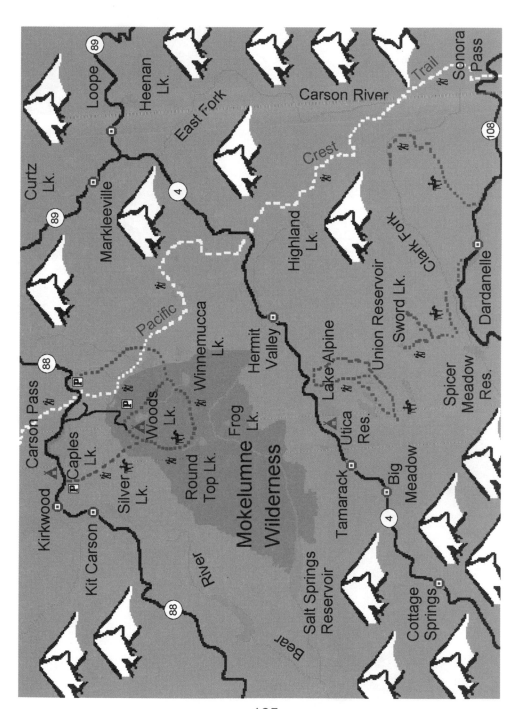

165

Mokelumne Wilderness

The Mokelumne River bisects remote mountainous terrain where elevations range from about 4,000 feet near Salt Springs Reservoir outside the southwest corner to over 10,000 feet near Carson Pass.

Shallow valleys lying north of Mokelumne Peak hide many small lakes where the fishing is often worth the hike. The fishing can also be good in the Mokelumne River.

However, the river canyon is extremely rugged with poison oak growing in profusion along the banks. Glaciers smoothed the area, leaving the well-placed trails relatively easy to hike. In spring and summer, several large meadows scattered throughout the wild land bloom with a riot of wildflower color.

Firewood is scarce in the Carson Pass area, and fires not are allowed in many sections. By late summer, water often becomes hard to find in the more remote regions. Permits are required for overnight visits between April 1 and November 30.

The Carson Pass trail to Winnemucca Lake is an easy 2.5 miles with great views. Winnemucca Lake to Round Top Lake is a steeper 1 mile trek into higher elevations approaching Round Top Peak. The Woods Lake trail is a 1.5 mile moderate hike that leads you into the cool forest and opens up to magnificent, flowering meadows in mid-July and August. The Lost Cabin Mine Trail is a steep 1.9 mile trail offering awesome views of the Sierra Nevada back country.

| Calaveras Ranger District |
| (209) 795-1381 |

166

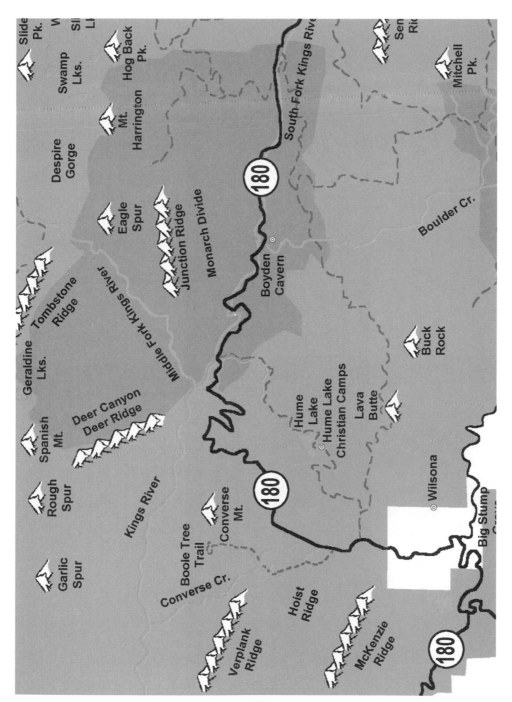

Monarch Wilderness

Monarch Wilderness amply lives up to its regal name. Few areas of the United States can boast such an abundance of extravagant mountain scenery.

Views from Spanish Mountain may be among the best in the world. This wildland is steep and rugged, with high ridges standing above deep canyons. Mountain meadows, numerous streams, shallow lakes, and spectacular multicolored rock formations throughout the Wilderness add to its wonder.

Kings River Ranger District
(559) 855-8321

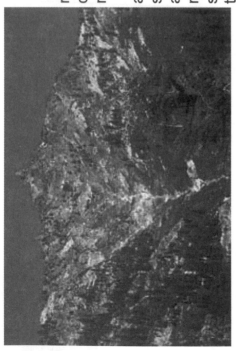

Elevations range from about 2,000 feet on the banks of the South Fork of the Kings River to 11,077 feet on Hogback Peak. Brush and oak woodlands cover the lower elevations, giving way to pine and red fir, and, finally, giant sequoias in the higher country.

The ragged, brushy terrain in the northwest portion has two loop trails, as well as trails leading into the King Canyon Park back country, and travel is extremely difficult. Trails in the southern area are mostly steep and strenuous. The Deer Cove Trail from Highway 180 climbs 3,000' in about 4 miles. This is a hike that is to be to avoided during midday.

Kanawyer Trail terminates at the Kings River. Since this is a very primitive area, it is important to check with the Rangers before going in for current conditions and hazards. There are a number of streams as well as the Kings River in which to fish. Be sure to treat the water before drinking it. The recommended procedure is to heat water to a rolling boil for five minutes. Wilderness Permits are required, but no visitor quotas are in effect. Always travel safely.

168

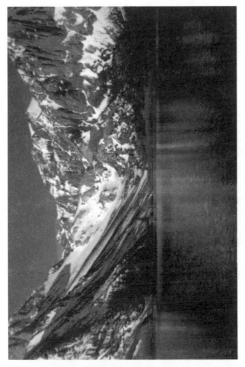

Mono County

From the high desert to the craggy peaks of the Sierra Nevada, across alpine lakes and lush meadows, along meandering streams and filled with abundant wildlife and spectacular flowers, Mono County is referred to as a "national park grandeur with gates."

Your senses will come alive with each changing season. Wildflowers burst forth in the spring. Mountain lakes beckon all summer. The autumn treats you to golden colors and crisp air. Winter calls with a promise of great skiing, a warm fireplace and beautiful scenery.

Mono County

Monitor Pass 89
Topaz Lake
Topaz
Golden Gate Mine
395
Coleville
Sonora Pass 108
Devil's Gate
Walker River
Hunewell Sawmill
Bridgeport Reservoir
Bridgeport
Bodie Ghost Town
Bodie and Benton Railroad
Twin Lakes
Dynamo Pond
Virginia Lakes
395
Lundy Lake
Lee Vining
Yosemite National Park
120
Mono Lake
Mono Craters
Black Lake
Benton
6
June Lake Loop
395
Ansel Adams Wilderness
Hot Creek
Owens River Gorge
120
Mammoth
Convict Lake
Crowley Lake
Tom's Place
John Muir Wilderness
McGee Creek
Rock Creek Lake
395

Visit Mono Lake, a 760,000 year old body of water. Be mystified by it's eerie limestone towers. You'll wonder at the variety of migratory birds that surround the lake and use the islands for nesting.

Take a day or two to walk through the old ghost town of Bodie. It is remarkable to see much of it still standing today. Peek through the school house windows and see the chalkboard, desks with inkwells and an old globe.

Relax in the warm waters of Hot Creek. Call ahead to schedule a tour of the geothermal plant along Highway 395, not far from the Mammoth area.

Fishing is remarkable. Opening day traditionally sees thousands of anglers flocking to Crowley Lake, hoping to net a giant trout! From the Owens River Gorge to the high elevation alpine lakes, fishermen will find many great spots to practice their art. Wintertime adds a mix of great activities for everyone. Mammoth Mountain Ski Area is known throughout the world as an excellent facility with all the amenities.

Mono County
Tourism Commission
(800) 845-7922
www.monocounty.org
CalTrans Road Conditions
(800) 427-7623
Emergencies
Dial 911

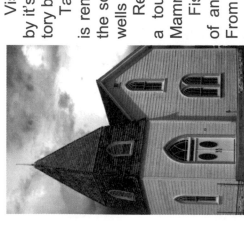

170

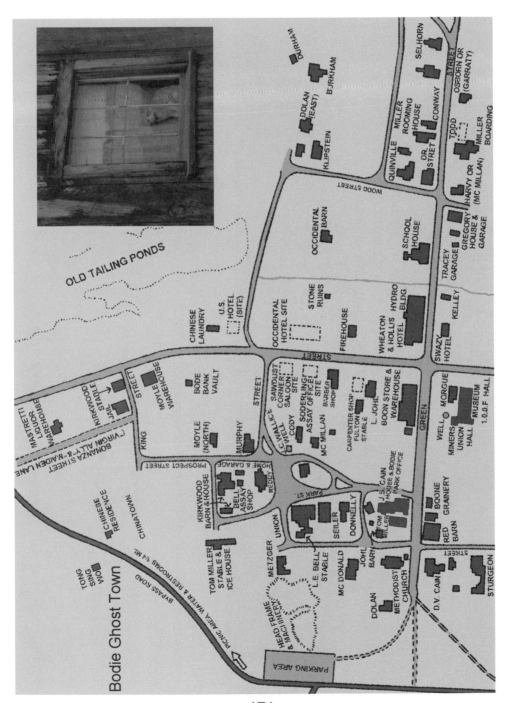

Bodie Ghost Town

OLD TAILING PONDS

TONG SING WO
CHINESE RESIDENCE
CHINATOWN
BYPASS ROAD
PICNIC AREA WATER & RESTROOMS 1/4 MI.

MASTRETTI LIQUOR WAREHOUSE
KIRKWOOD STABLE
JAIL
(VIRGIN ALLY? & MAIDEN LANE)
BONANZA ST STREET

KING STREET
MOYLE WAREHOUSE
BODE BANK VAULT
CHINESE LAUNDRY
U.S. HOTEL (SITE)

MOYLE (NORTH)
MURPHY STREET
PROSPECT STREET

KIRKWOOD BARN & HOUSE
BELL ASSAY SHOP
HOME & GARAGE
REDDY
C. WALLACE WELL
CODY
SODERLING' SAWDUST CORNER SALOON SITE
ASSAY OFFICE SITE
MC MILLAN
STREET

OCCIDENTAL HOTEL SITE
STONE RUINS
FIREHOUSE

OCCIDENTAL BARN

WOOD STREET

DURHAM
BJRKHAM
KLIPSTEIN
DOLAN (EAST)

QUINVILLE
MILLER ROOMING HOUSE
DR. STRET
CONWAY
SELHORN
STREET
OSBORN OR (GARRATY)
TODD
GREGORY (HARVY OR (MC MILLAN)
HOUSE & GARAGE
MILLER BOARDING

SCHOOL HOUSE

TRACEY GARAGE
SWAZY HOTEL
KELLEY
HYDRO BLDG
WHEATON & HOLLIS HOTEL

TOM MILLER STABLE & ICE HOUSE
METZGER
UNION
L.E. BELL STABLE
MC DONALD
SEILER
DONNELLY
J.S. CAIN HOUSE & BODIE PARK OFFICE
PARK ST.
TOM MILLER
JOHL BARN
DOLAN
METHODIST CHURCH
BOONE GRAINERY
RED BARN
D.V. CAIN
STURGEON
STREET

CARPENTER SHOP
FULTON STABLE
L. JOHL
BOON STORE & WAREHOUSE
BARBER SHOP

GREEN STREET

WELL
MORGUE
MUSEUM
MINERS UNION HALL
1.0.0.F. HALL

HEAD FRAME & MACHINERY
PARKING AREA

171

Bodie Ghost Town

Bodie was named after Waterman S. Body (also known as William S. Bodey) who discovered gold there in 1859. The change in spelling of the town's name has often been attributed to an illiterate sign painter, but in fact it was a deliberate change by the citizenry to insure proper pronunciation.

The town of Bodie rose to prominence with the decline of mining along the western slope of the Sierra Nevada. Prospectors crossing the eastern slope in 1859 to "see the Elephant" -

that is, search for gold - discovered what was to be the Comstock Lode at Virginia City, and started a wild rush to the surrounding high desert country.

Bodie became a boom town in 1877 and by 1879 Bodie boasted a population of about 10,000 with 2,000 buildings, and was second to none for wickedness, badmen, and "the worst climate out of doors".

One little girl, whose family was taking her to the remote and infamous town, wrote in her diary: "Good-bye God, I'm going to Bodie". The phrase came to be known throughout the west. Killings occurred with montonous regularity, sometimes becoming almost daily events. The fire bell, which tolled the ages of the deceased when they were buried, rang often and long.

Robberies, stage holdups, and street fights provided variety, and the town's 65 saloons offered many opportunities for relaxation after a hard days of work in the mines.

Bodie State Historic Park
(760) 647-6445

173

The Reverend F.M. Warrington saw it in 1881 as "a sea of sin, lashed by the tempest of lust and passion."

The town was more known for its wild living than for its big gold resources. Every other building on the mile long main street was a saloon. Seven breweries worked day and night. The whiskey was brought in by horse carriages, 100 barrels at a time. The boom was over in four short years and by 1882, Bodie was in the grips of decline.

Then the rich mines played out and the mining companies went bankrupt. Two fires, one in 1892 and another in 1932, ravaged the business district. Bodie faded into a ghost town during the 1940's. It became a State Historic Park in 1962, managed in a state of arrested decay. Today, with less than 10% of the town still standing, it is still the largest ghost town in the western United States, and what is left looks much the same as it did over 50 years ago.

Nearly everyone has heard about the infamous "Badman from Bodie." Some historians say that he was Tom Adams. Others say his name was Washoe Pete. More than likely, he was a composite. Bad men, like bad whiskey and bad climate, were endemic to the area.

Whatever the case, the streets are quiet now. Bodie still has its wicked climate, but with the possible exception of an occasional ghostly visitor, its badmen are all in their graves.

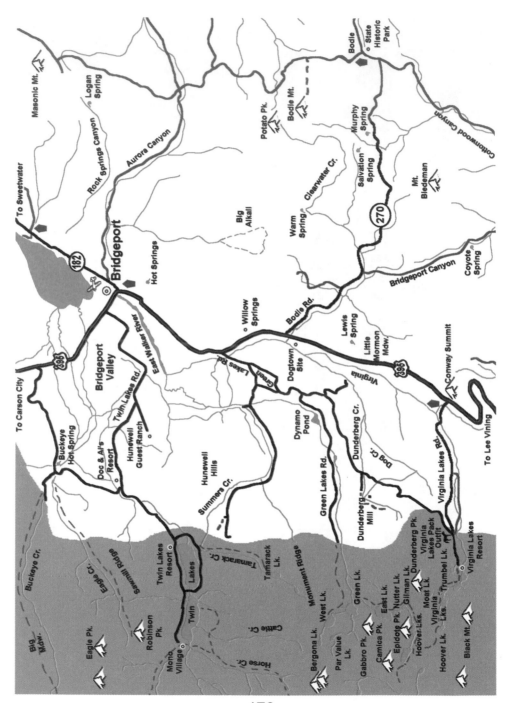

Bridgeport

Considered by many as a hidden paradise in the Eastern Sierra, Bridgeport is a gateway to many fantastic vacation spots under the watchful eye of the Sawtooth Ridge. Great fishing is available nearby at a number of lakes, creeks, streams and the Walker River.

There are many areas close by for camping, hiking, backpacking, horseback riding and sightseeing. Fishing is excellent. The California Record Trout was taken at a lake just a few miles away.

Bridgeport hosts a number of events each year, including a rodeo and a black powder shooting contest.

There are ghost towns, a dude ranch and hot springs just minutes away.

Drive up to Devil's Gate and learn about John C. Fremont winter crossing and look for his lost cannon. Go see the Dynamo Ponds from which electricity was generated to send power to Bodie in the old days. The engineers insisted the power poles used to carry the electrical lines were set in an absolutely straight line so the electricity would not fly off the wire on a curve! Obviously, this was in an era when the use of electricity was a very new concept.

177

During the spring and summer, visit the museum. It's set in the old school house.

There are a variety of facilities for lodging, including bed & breakfast inns, restaurants with great food and all the services you may need while traveling.

A drive up to Twin Lakes is scenic and the view of the Sawtooth Mountains is awe inspiring! The winter months feature some beautifully snow covered mountains reaching for the very sky. But, no matter how long you stay or what you actually do, you'll want to come back.

Bridgeport Chamber
(760) 932-7500
Bridgport Ranger Station
(760) 932-7070
Virginia Creek Settlement
(760) 932-7780
Falling Rock Marina
(760) 932-7001
Leavitt Meadows Pack Outfit
(530) 495-2257

Convict Lake

After spending a long day drowning worms, backpacking, taking a canoe ride, hiking or horseback riding through the beautiful back country, you can treat yourself to a truly memorable dining experience at what has become one of the finest restaurants between Reno and Los Angeles.

Choose a cozy cabin for a few days. Take a picture or two of the raccoon visitors you may have. Or you can pick a site at the campground. There are 88 sites on a first-come, first-served basis. An RV dump station for those with RVs.

The store is completely stocked with all the vacation supplies, fishing tackle, gift items and more. The marina has boats for rent, including party barges, mooring facilities and fuel for watercraft.

The riding stables is open from May through October and has saddle horses available for hour rides. They also have a lead horse program for kids seven and under.

Trailheads lead to the John Muir and Pacific Crest Trails. You can visit the high country lakes, streams and scenery that are truly wonderful to experience.

You can arrange for a tour of a geothermal plant, near Mammoth, see the Hot Springs Fish Hatchery and relax in the hot springs.

Take a short drive to Mammoth and treat the kids to a first run movie.

In 1871, 29 prisoners escaped from Carson City. Six went south and killed mail carrier Billy Poor, near Aurora. A posse found them on the shore of Monte Diablo Lake, now known as Convict Lake.

Gunfire erupted. Two of the posse were killed, including Robert Morrison, at for whom Mt. Morrison, at the lake's south shore was named. The convicts escaped. Two were caught later in Round Valley near Bishop and were hung by citizens.

Things to Do!

There is an abundance of things to see and activities to do in this area, so here's a little map that will help you find how to get to all these places, well known or not!

When you visit Hot Creek and walk down to the water, be careful, the water can change temperature rather quickly due to geothermal activity far below the surface!

Stop at Tom's Place for good meal or favorite libation.

You can arrange for a tour of the geothermal plant by calling the facility and requesting a tour.

Use caution during bad weather, road conditions can turn dangerous quickly.

There are wonderful folks all around the Sierra Nevada who will help make your visit a memorable one!

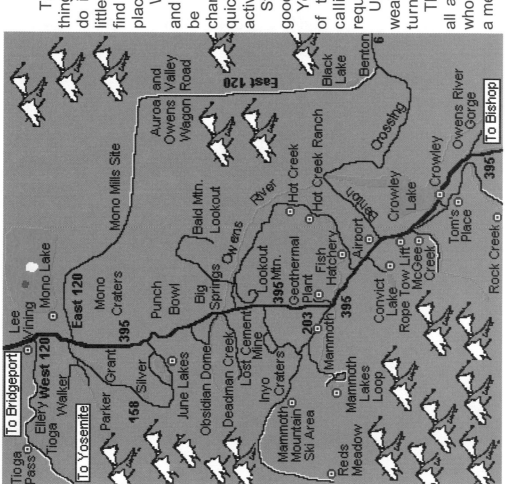

Crowley Lake

Over 6,000 fisherman drive hundreds of miles, many towing their boats, and descend upon the lake each year for the opening day of the trout fishing season.

This phenomena has been going on for decades. What do these people must know? Let's review. Crowley offers up some good sized fish.

This great expanse of water is well known for "giant" trout. If you're planning on fishing "opening" day on Crowley, make reservations for lodging or camping early!

But you have to get there late spring or early summer, because the lake gets too warm to produce good trout fishing by mid summer. You can also try fishing on the Owens River.

Later in the summer, you'll see folks water skiing over the surface. Sailors and wind surfers enjoy the gentle breezes, while others go swimming or test their jet ski skills!

182

Devil's Post Pile National Monument

Past Mammoth Lakes and the spacious Mammoth Mountain ski area is the road to Red's Meadow. Here you'll find a geologic formation called "the Postpile". It is the world's finest example of unusual columnar basalt. Its columns of lava, with their four to seven sides, display a honeycomb pattern of order and harmony. This is a very interesting pile of rocks! Bring your hiking shoes, water and a snack, along with film and camera!

A shuttle bus runs into Reds Meadows from the Mammoth Mountain Ski area.

It's only accessible May to October.

Devil's Postpile
www.nps.gov/depo

183

Mammoth-Pacific Geothermal Complex

This unique facility captures geothermal hot water to help fuel three power plants that combine to provide the energy needs for about 40,000 homes. The water heats a liquid in a piping system that is fed into the main plant to keep the turbines running.

Additionally, the complex provides an economic benefit to the community and the county, while capturing a clean, reusable energy resource. It is actually displacing the need to import 500,000 barrels of oil annually. You can tour by reservation.

**Mammoth Pacific
Geothermal Complex**
(760) 934-4893

Hot Creek - A Warm Springs and Fly Fishing Mecca

Access to Hot Creek is open daily from sunrise to sunset. The ground can be very unstable and you must stay on the sidewalk for your own safety.

Dogs must be leashed and in your grasp. Please keep an eye on young children to avoid potential accidents. Glass containers are not allowed. Soap and shampoo pollute the water and are not allowed. Remember to pack out what you bring in.

Earthquakes are common in this area and can cause drastic changes in the underground plumbing. During the earthquake swarms in 1980s, there were sudden geyser eruptions at Hot Creek, and overnight appearances of new hot springs and changes in creek bed, shoreline and water temperature. It is suggested to stay out of the water after such an event.

Hot Creek is designated as an official Wild Trout Stream. It is a very popular area for fly fishing. Only naturally reproducing trout exist in the stream.

A tiny mosquito eating fish, called Gambusia, is seen in areas that the water is very warm. You'll also see the Owens Sucker and Tui Chub.

Hot Creek Fish Hatchery

An ideal environment for trout development is provided by the warm springs of Hot Creek. You can visit this interesting facility. It is operated by the California Department of Fish and Game. It is open daily, year round.

RAINBOW TROUT
Salmo gairdneri

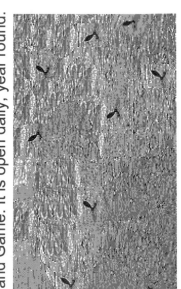

186

Hunewill
Guest Ranch

is located just east of Yosemite National Park in the green, mountainous Bridgeport Valley of California. The Hunewill Ranch is a family owned and operated outfit where great horseback riding is the featured attraction. You'll love riding your horse through this 26,000 acre expanse of cool, lush meadow, bordered by timbered peaks. Hunewill offers you a full ranch experience, including evening activities such as talent night, family dance night, barbecues on the creek, or watching as young foals and yearlings are being gentled. There is world class trout fishing in the nearby East Walker River, and in the many lakes and streams in the adjacent Toiyabe National Forest. Home style meals are served in the dining room in the founder's Victorian ranch house. You'll stay in comfortable cottages near the horse pasture; allowing you to watch the horses come thundering in early each morning. The Hunewill Ranch was founded in 1861 by Napoleon Bonaparte Hunewill and his wife Esther. In the 1930's LeNoe and Stanley Hunewill started the Hunewill Guest Ranch. Today Hunewill Guest Ranch is still a working cattle ranch with 1200 cows and 120 horses,, as well as 60 sheep, 35 llamas and 4 pigs. Naturally, cattle work is something that you can participate in. The traditional fall cattle drive to the winter ranch in Nevada covers 60 miles. For a vacation experience suited to families, singles or couples you won't find a friendlier place. If you want home-style meals, wide open space, great riding and lasting friendships then Hunewill Guest Ranch is the vacation for you.

187

Winter (775) 465-2201 Summer (760) 932-7710
www.hunewillranch.com

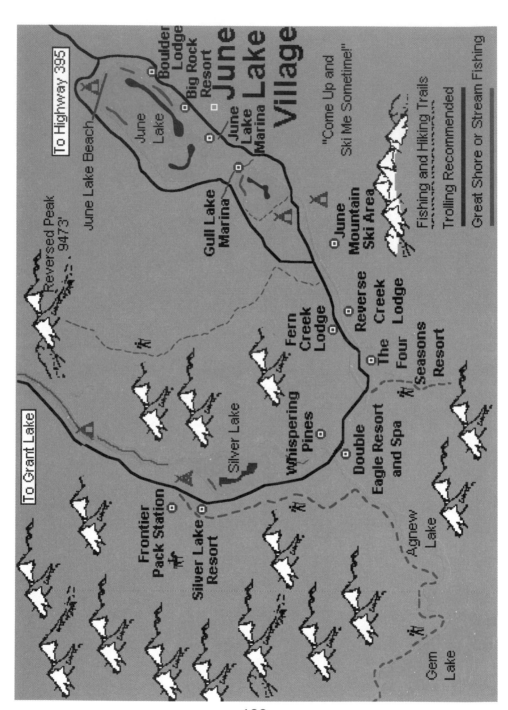

To Highway 395

June Lake Beach

Reversed Peak
9473'

Boulder Lodge

Big Rock Resort

June Lake

June Lake Marina

June Lake Village

"Come Up and Ski Me Sometime!"

Gull Lake Marina

June Mountain Ski Area

Fishing and Hiking Trails

Trolling Recommended

Great Shore or Stream Fishing

To Grant Lake

Fern Creek Lodge

Reverse Creek Lodge

The Four Seasons Resort

Whispering Pines

Silver Lake

Double Eagle Resort and Spa

Frontier Pack Station

Silver Lake Resort

Agnew Lake

Gem Lake

June Lakes

Located in the Eastern Sierras, between the Mammoth Lake area and Lee Vining, the June Lakes Loop is just an hour's drive through Tioga Pass from Tuolumne Meadows in Yosemite National Park.

Here you'll find four mountain lakes, situated along Highway 158, and there's a lot more up the various trails leading to the Ansel Adams Wilderness.

June Lake has been referred to as "a scenic adventure for the senses." During the spring, summer and fall you can take a saddle

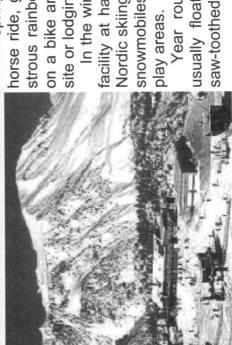

horse ride, go hiking, try for monstrous rainbow trout, ride the loop on a bike and relax at your campsite or lodging accommodation.

In the winter, there's a great ski facility at hand offering alpine and Nordic skiing, ice climbing, trails for snowmobiles and family fun snow play areas.

Year round, white clouds are usually floating over the majestic saw-toothed Carson Peak.

There are a variety of resorts, lodges, motels, plus bed and breakfast inns in which to spend a night or two. Naturally, you can stay longer!

Enjoy your meals in the many restaurants and have a drink or two in one of the local taverns.

There are marinas with boat rentals, repair facilities, mooring, fuel, bait and tackle.

The grocery and sporting goods stores can make sure you have everything you need to make your stay an enjoyable one!

190

During your stay, take time to drive over to Mono Lake. Pack a lunch, bring lots of drinking water and a pair of good walking shoes. Start at the Visitor's Center and learn more about this ancient body of water. Then pick a spot and get a closer look. Bring a camera.

The little community of Lee Vining has an interesting Visitor's Center, and a museum, just off the main highway. You can also take a drive up Highway 120 toward Ticga Pass. The overview of the high desert and the White Mountains is incredible.

Tioga Pass has several lakes in the general vicinity, plus trails to points of interest. Old Bennettville, once a home to silver mining operations, is a very interesting place to visit. It's an easy hike and well worth it.

If you have time, a short drive to Saddlebag Lake will reward you with great photo opportunities.

Frontier Pack Train
(760) 648-7701
www.frontierpacktrain.com
Grant Lake Marina
(760) 648-7964
June Lake Loop Chamber
(760) 648-7584
www.junelake.com
June Lake Marina
(760) 648-7726
www.junelakemarina.com
June Mountain Ski Area
www.junemountain.com
(760) 648-7357

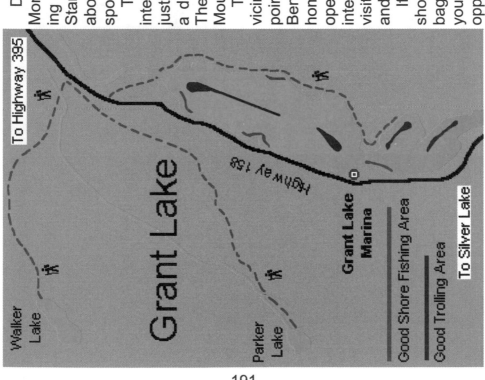

Grant Lake

To Highway 395

Walker Lake

Parker Lake

Highway 158

Grant Lake Marina

Good Shore Fishing Area

Good Trolling Area

To Silver Lake

191

Lee Vining

Near the intersection of Highways 120 and 395, this is a great place to decide which way you want to go. Tuolumne Meadows, Yosemite and the recreation area around Tioga Pass are west on Highway 120; the June Lakes Loop, the Mammoth Lakes area, and Bishop are south on Highway 395; the ghost town of Bodie, the Bridgeport recreation area and Walker Pass are north on Highway 395.

You'll definitely want to visit scenic Mono Lake, a ancient body of water surrounded by mysteries. There's an informative Visitor's Center just up the road. It's a great place to spend a day exploring and have a picnic.

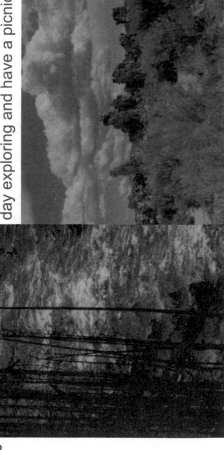

The ghost town of Bodie is another place with historical significance to visit. On the road to Bridgeport, the once thriving gold mining town is about 45 minutes off Highway 395. There are more than 50 structures still standing. Some are almost in the same condition as the day the last folks left! This area is not accessible in the winter due to snow conditions.

Lee Vining has motels, an RV park, bed & breakfast inns, good places to eat, markets, sporting good stores and antique dealers!

Lee Vining Chamber
(760) 647-6629
www.leevining.com
Lee Vining Ranger
(760) 647-3040

Lundy Lake

Approximately 12 miles northwest of Lee Vining you'll find this beautiful lake. Lots of hungry trout await you!

Stay at the resort that has 15 housekeeping cabins. There are RV and tent sites, with flush toilets, showers, a laundry, boat rentals and a general store.

It's open from late spring through Oct.

Aside from fishing, you can try one of the many hiking and backpacking trails that lead into the Hoover Wilderness. Enjoy the scenic vistas while you relax with a good book. Bring a nice warm jacket, the evenings can get rather cool.

Lundy Lake Resort
(626) 309 0415

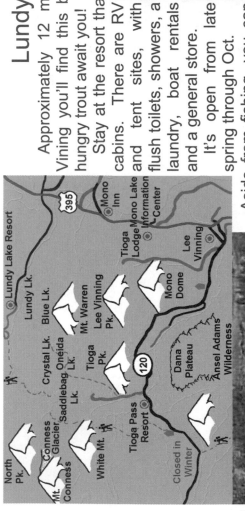

194

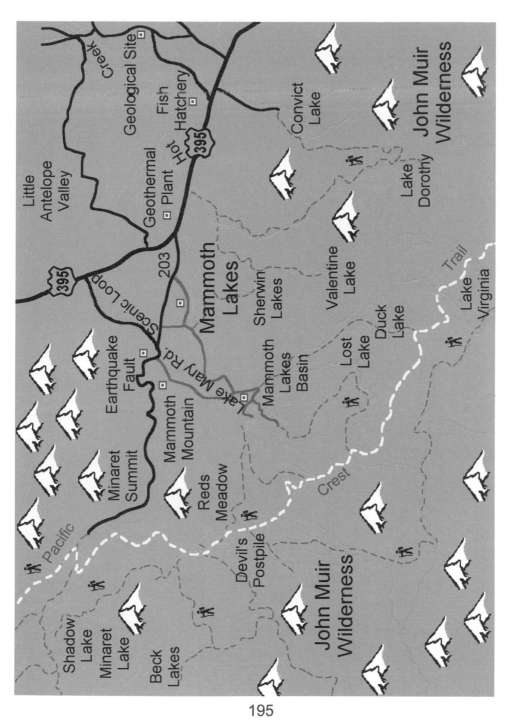

Little Antelope Valley

Creek

Geological Site

Fish Hatchery

Hot

Convict Lake

John Muir Wilderness

Geothermal Plant

395

395

Scenic Loop

203

Mammoth Lakes

Sherwin Lakes

Lake Dorothy

Valentine Lake

Lake Virginia

Trail

Earthquake Fault

Lake Mary Rd.

Mammoth Lakes Basin

Lost Lake

Duck Lake

Minaret Summit

Mammoth Mountain

Reds Meadow

Crest

Devil's Postpile

Pacific

Shadow Lake

Minaret Lake

Beck Lakes

John Muir Wilderness

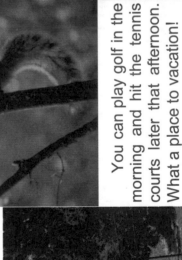

Mammoth

One of the premier vacation destinations in the world, this community really does offer something for everyone. There are exciting activities for young and old, three hundred and sixty five days a year. And every four years when there's a Leap Year, with an extra day, there are great things to do on that day too!

Aside from the traditional Sierra outdoor sports like fishing, hiking and mountain biking, plus rock climbing, horseback riding and the host of winter activities, there's more!

You can play golf in the morning and hit the tennis courts later that afternoon. What a place to vacation!

196

You can treat the kids to a first run movie or let them enjoy an afternoon or evening at the arcade.

A variety of special events is offered each year, including recitals, jazz festivals, musical concerts, art shows and others. As you would imagine, the choice of lodging is immense.

The same holds true for dining. From fast food favorites to elegant restaurants, featuring almost every style of cuisine, you surely can find something to ease your appetite.

Anything you need for your trip you could actually buy right here. From supermarkets to swank clothing stores and well outfitted sporting goods outlets, if you need it, it's near by.

Mammoth Lakes
www.mammothlakes.com
Mammoth Lakes Visitors Bureau
(888) GO-Mammoth
www.visitmammoth.com
Mammoth Lakes Pack Outfit
(760) 934-2434
Mammoth Ranger District
(760) 924-5500

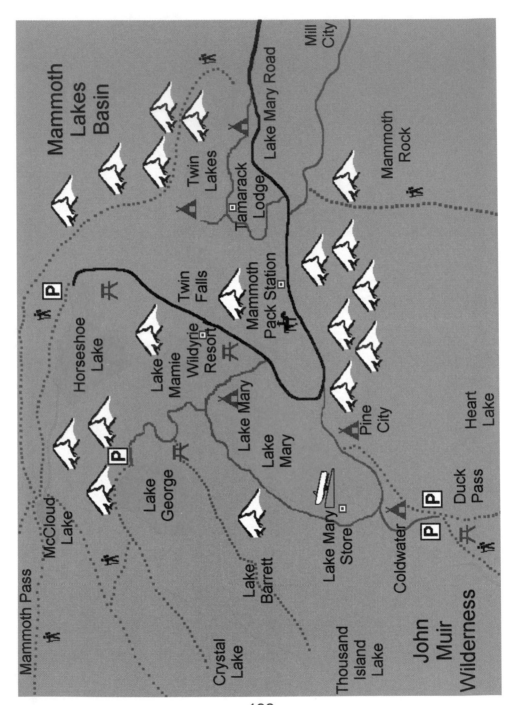

Mammoth Lakes Basin

Mill City

Lake Mary Road

Twin Lakes

Tamarack Lodge

Mammoth Rock

Twin Falls

Mammoth Pack Station

Horseshoe Lake

Lake Mamie

Wildyrie Resort

Lake Mary

Lake Mary

Pine City

Heart Lake

McCloud Lake

Lake George

Lake Mary Store

Duck Pass

Coldwater

Lake Barrett

Crystal Lake

Thousand Island Lake

John Muir Wilderness

Mammoth Pass

Mammoth Lakes Basin

Camping, fishing, hiking and horseback riding are very popular in this beautiful area. A favorite with families, there are boat rentals, boat launching facilities, great food and lodging. Day rides and other activities are offered by the pack outfit.

McCloud Lake is a short, easy hike from the trailhead at Horseshoe Lake. The Red's Meadows area and the John Muir Wilderness are also accessible from trails that rim the Mammoth Lakes Basin.

The Ranger Station in Mammoth can issue you a Wilderness Permit for extended back country stays.

Lake Mary Store
(760) 934-5353
Mammoth Lakes Pack Outfit
(760) 934-2434
Tamarack Lodge
(760) 934-5353
www.tamaracklodge.com
Wildyrie Resort
(760) 934-2444

Mammoth Mountain

With over 3,500 acres of terrain with wide open bowls, steep chutes, tree-lined cruisers, terrain parks and half pipes, this is a wonderful world class ski area that draws skiers and riders of all ages and abilities.

There are more than 150 trails with names like Hangman's Hollow and Climax, Broadway and Mambo, and Hansel and Gretel. Thirty lifts serve you and allow you to quickly move between Main Lodge, Canyon Lodge and Little Eagle. This area is blessed with mountains of snow each year, which allows for a long winter season.

The Mammoth Sports School prides itself on providing the best techniques to lead you into a lifelong passion for skiing and boarding. The sun shines at least 300 days annually. Après ski can take place at most anytime. There is a variety of enticing on-mountain locations.

Mammoth's only slopeside, full-service resort hotel at the Main Lodge, is the Mammoth Mountain Inn.

It features 213 hotel rooms and suites with kitchens to entice visitors from around the world to relax and enjoy themselves.

Mammoth Mountain operates a shuttle service to the scenic Reds Meadow area during the fishing and hiking season. You should hike to Rainbow Falls and to Devils Postpile.

Mammoth Mountain Ski Area
(760) 934-0628
www.mammothmountain.com
Mammoth Mountain Inn
(760) 934-2581

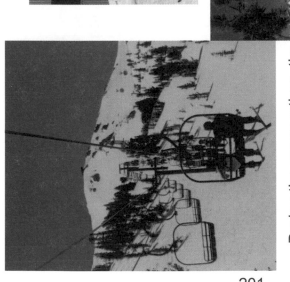

During the summertime, the ski runs become mountain bike trails. The lifts now take you to the top, but the ride down is a much different thrill than it's winter counterpart.

If you're just interested in a great view of the Crowley Lake area from afar, take a gondola ride to the summit. The scenery is very spectacular.

McGee Creek

Wonderful places to fish, camp and hike await you in the McGee Creek area. Just a short drive off Highway 395, near Crowley Lake, takes you into a breathtaking wilderness through which McGee Creek flows.

It takes you to one of the most colorful canyons in the state, McGee Canyon. Here are breathtaking colors and geological formations that will amaze you at every turn.

There are campgrounds at the McGee Creek Trailhead. McGee Creek Pack Station is close by. Lee and Jennifer Roeser, along with their staff, can provide you with day rides or back country pack trips.

Destinations include Round Lake, which is considered perfect for families. Kids will enjoy swimming in the warm lake, exploring meadows, and first-time fishing in the lakes or close-by McGee Creek. Campsites on the lake or stream also offer a central locality to other lakes and points of interest in the canyon.

Big McGee Lake is situated in a high glacial moraine, surrounded by exquisite meadows, peaks and waterfalls.

Grass and Steelhead Lakes are nestled in a quiet side canyon, and offer fishing for rainbow, golden, and Eastern brook. You can take an easy hike to nearby Meadow, Gold, or Crocker Lakes. Steelhead Lake is considered by many as possibly the most beautiful lake you will ever see. You can hike along at your own pace, unencumbered by a heavy backpack, or you may prefer to ride a gentle animal, (horses or mules).

There are lots of options you can choose as you plan to travel to a lake or meadow and set up camp for 4 or 5 days. You can also travel from camp to camp for as many days as you wish.

If you really want to travel in style, you can hire a mountain chef to accompany you, leaving lots of time to do what you prefer!

The days are usually in the mid 70s, with the evenings becoming quite cool. Remember that the weather can change rapidly, so always pack accordingly!

203

McGee Creek Pack Station
(800) 854-7407
www.mcgeecreekpackstation.com
Lee Roeser and pack animals.

Mono Craters

East of Highway 395, south of Mono Lake, are a range of volcanic cones that attract the eye, not only on account of their height and the symmetry of their curving slopes of light gray lapilli, but also because they form so striking an exception to the prevailing mountain forms in view.

Their shapes are almost perfect and the eye lingers about their summits in half expectation of seeing wreaths of vapor or the lurid light of molten lava ascending from their throats. The Mono Craters, stretching to the south of Mono erupted recently in geologic time and are some of the more obvious volcanic features at Mono Lake along with Black Point and the Negit Island volcanoes. The volcanic chain stretchs 10 miles north to south, and tops 9,000 ft.

It may be the youngest volcanic mountain range in North America. The last eruption in the Mono Craters chain nearly 700 years ago at Panum Crater. Odds are the Mono Craters will erupt again. Imagine a volcanic eruption 2,500 times greater than the Mt. St. Helens blast of 1980! Twenty miles south of present-day Mono lies the northern edge of Long Valley Caldera. The Long Valley eruption, 760,000 years ago, blasted more than 150 cubic miles of earth and ash skyward, burying much of the region in hundreds of feet of volcanic debris. Ash fell as far east as Nebraska.

The earth surface collapsed more than one mile deep following the eruption, forming a 200 square mile depression, called Long Valley Caldera. Today, it's part of a volcanic complex stretching from Mammoth Mountain to Mono Lake.

204

Mono Lake
A Photographer's Dream

Mono Lake is an oasis in the dry Great Basin and a vital habitat for millions of migratory and nesting birds.

Geologists have determined the age of Mono Lake from the Long Valley eruption.

In 1908, oil prospectors, crilling for oil on Paoha Island, discovered an ash layer from the Long Valley eruption beneath hundreds of feet of lake sediment.

Beyond the ash layer was more

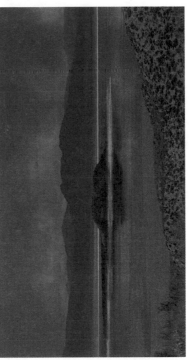

lake sediment, which showed the secret to its age. It's had water since the Long Valley eruption 760,000 years ago, making it one of country's oldest.

Mono Lake is a salty, alkaline inland sea home to brine shrimp, alkali flies, and the millions of birds that depend on them. Flowing down from the Sierra Nevada escarpment, freshwater streams create a different habitat where aspens, willows, and cottonwoods grow.

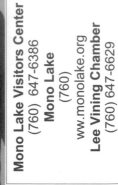

The Mono Basin is home to millions of birds representing over 300 species. Most are migratory, and over 100 species nest here as well.

The Mono Basin watershed has a variety of habitats, and each supports its own collection of bird species as well as birds commonly seen throughout the Basin.

In the 1970s, it became evident that Mono Land was drying up. For years, water was taken from the Basin by Los Angeles area consumers. Twenty-one years ago a suit was filed against Los Angeles Department of Water and Power on behalf of the Public Trust value of Mono Lake.

Today Mono's creeks are full of water, the lake is at its highest point in almost 30 years, and the City of Los Angeles has one of the lowest per capita water use levels in the State.

Be sure to tour the Mono Lake Visitor's Center!

206

Red's Meadow

Off Highway 395, thru Mammoth Lakes and past the famous Mammoth Mountain Ski Area, you'll catch a glimpse of the Minarets, a distinguished mountain range. You then begin a descent into beautiful Red's Meadow.

This is a very popular area and is controlled by the Forest Service to avoid overcrowding. You'll need to make a camping reservation if you plan to stay in the area overnight. If you have booked a pack trip with a pack station, you can continue into Red's Meadow. There is a shuttle service, run by Mammoth Mountain, that will take you into the area and back out for day hikes, fishing excursions and just to explore this beautiful back country.

Red's Meadow a land of crystal-clear streams and emerald lakes, of vast, unspoiled virgin forests, touched only by mountain trails. This is a paradise for the photographer, fisherman, hunter and those who seek rest and solitude.

Here the entire family can enjoy a great vacation. Spend a day visiting the Devil's Postpile National Monument and another hiking to the majestic Rainbow Falls on the San Joaquin River. Picturesque Sotcher Lake is within walking distance.

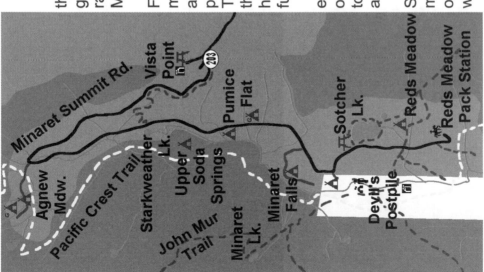

Soda Springs, Hot Springs, Minaret Falls, the San Joaquin River and the Muir Trail are a few of the enjoyable attractions of this fascinating area located between the John Muir and Ansel Adams Wilderness areas. Yosemite National Park is nearby for extended hikes or pack trips.

Cabins, great food, a soda fountain, groceries and fishing tackle are available at the well-stocked Red's Meadow General Store and Mule House cafe.

Horseback excursions and pack trips are available to many exciting destinations at the Red's Meadow or Agnew Meadows Pack Stations.

There is an excess of 100 lakes and many miles of streams within a day's ride. Secluded camp spots and seldom-visited lakes and streams can make an excellent place to relax and enjoy your vacation.

Red's Meadow Pack Station
(800) 292-7758 (760) 934-2345
www.reds-meadow.com
Camping Reservations
(877) 444-6777
www.reserveusa.com

Rock Creek

Catch the turn off to this secluded section of the Sierra Nevada near Tom's Place on Highway 395. You'll head west into the brush and you'll wind your way along scenic Rock Creek into some of the most beautiful countryside the mountains have to offer.

There is trailhead parking in several spots as you head back towards the Resort and Pack Station. In the winter, you can park in any of them and try cross country skiing, go snow shoeing or play in the snow with the kids.

The paved road in this canyon ends at 10,200', at a trailhead leading to Little Lakes Valley.

This area is fantastic for day hikes, steam or lake fishing, camping and overnight trips into the John Muir Wilderness.

There are lots of campsites are in the area, as well as the Resort.

If you enjoy solitude, your stay in the Rock Creek area will be perfect for you. Listen to the creek as you drift off to sleep.

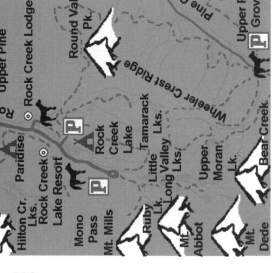

209

If you're sleeping outdoors, you'll struggle to keep your eyes open watching the twinkling stars.

Aside from the usual activities you can enjoy on vacation, you can try your hand at rock climbing. The folks at the Resort can point out some suitable crags for beginners and advanced climbers.

Most locals say the stream fishing is excellent, and even better out on the lake in a boat.

Food, boat rentals, fishing tackle, groceries and cabins are yours for the asking, plus a reasonable fee! For those interested in heading into the wilderness on horseback, the pack station has a seasoned staff to help you enjoy your experience. You can choose from a hour's ride or spend several days in the saddle in the backcountry.

If you enjoy mountain biking, you can always park at Tom's Place and follow the creek all the way back to the Lodge.

Have lunch and a cool drink before heading back to the car.

Mammoth Ranger District
(760) 924-5500
Rock Creek Lodge
(760) 935-4311
www.rockcreeklodge.com
Rock Creek Pack Station
(760) 935-4493
www.rockcreekpackstation.com

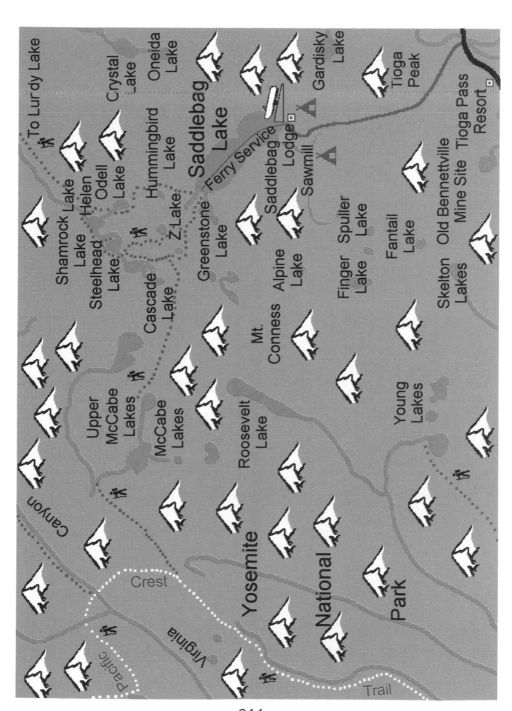

To Lurdy Lake

Crystal Lake

Oneida Lake

Gardisky Lake

Tioga Peak

Tioga Pass Resort

Shamrock Lake

Steelhead Lake

Helen Odell Lake

Hummingbird Lake

Saddlebag Lake

Ferry Service

Z Lake

Greenstone Lake

Saddlebag Lodge

Sawmill

Finger Lake

Spuller Lake

Fantail Lake

Old Bennettville Mine Site

Skelton Lakes

Cascade Lake

Alpine Lake

Mt. Conness

Upper McCabe Lakes

McCabe Lakes

Roosevelt Lake

Young Lakes

Canyon

Crest

Virginia

Pacific

Yosemite

National

Park

Trail

211

Saddlebag Lake

This lake, at 10,283 feet has the distinction of being the highest one you can drive to the in U.S, and the air is definitely thinner. You'll walk a bit slower for the first day or so. But, it's well worth it.

Open from June to October, the resort offers boat rentals, water-taxi service between the north and south ends of the lake, bait and tackle, fishing licenses, souvenirs, supplies, and some mouth watering home

Saddlebag Lake Resort
(760) 932-7751

cooked meals. The friendly folks at the resort will gladly provide helpful information on fishing, hiking and obtaining Wilderness Permits for those who plan to stay out in the back country overnight.

The area surrounding the lake used to be a tungsten mining operation. You can still see where some of the operations took place. At the far end of the lake, there is a trail that takes you to a loop of about 10 lakes that you can walk around on a day trip, or stay overnight. There are lots of Golden Trout to be taken. You'll want to take water, a hearty snack and a good sized lunch. Wear comfortable hiking shoes. If you're only planning to stay the day, be sure to catch the last boat taxi back across the lake to avoid an extra mile or so back to the main parking area. Early mornings and late evenings are cold, be sure you have a good jacket and warm bedroll. Speaking of bed time, take advantage of this altitude to check out the heavens.

Tioga Pass

One of three major gateways from the western Sierra Nevada to the eastern side of the mountains, Highway 120 runs through scenic Tioga Pass, the home of many beautiful sites and several things to do.

Lee Vining is on the eastern side of this portal, with Yosemite National Park's Tuolumne Meadows on the west. Snow conditions force the closure of this transition during the winter, usually from November to late May.

Lakes, streams, hiking trails, ruins of old mining towns and more await you here at Tioga Pass. It's a very picturesque place. The fishing is a good at both the lakes here on the road, Tioga and Ellery.

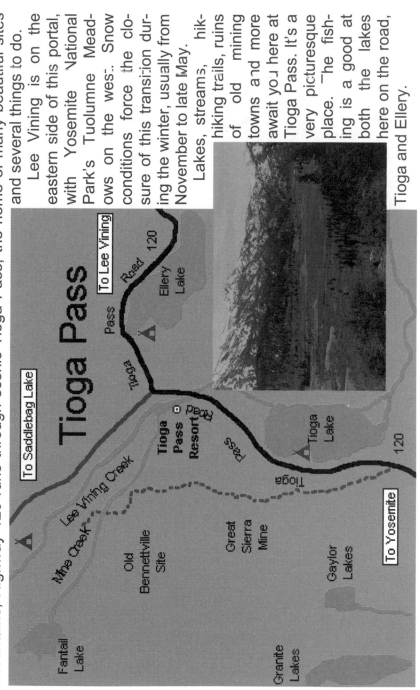

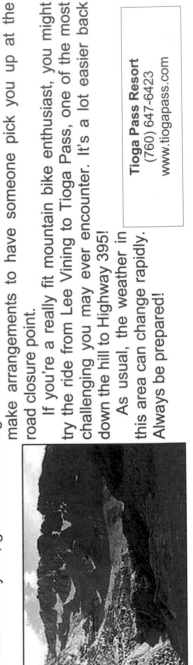

Saddlebag Lake, a two mile trek up a bumpy dirt road, is a jumping off point for overnight hikers who want to head to the backcountry of Yosemite or the Hoover Wilderness. There's a ferry service to take you across the lake to the trailhead.

Lake Ellery and Tioga Lake offer up excellent fishing. There are a number of scenic campsites in the vicinity, plus day use picnic areas.

The Tioga Pass Resort has rustic cabins and old style hospitality. The food is excellent. Try a bowl of their famous chili on a cloudy summer's day, along with a hot cup of chocolate. If you're partial to breakfast as your favorite daily meal, this is the place to eat!

The store is completely stocked for the fisherman, camper and backpacker. There's a lovely gift shop and fuel for your vehicle, camp stove or lanterns. In the winter, folks come to cross country ski, go snow shoeing and ride their snowmobiles. Since the road is closed, you make arrangements to have someone pick you up at the road closure point.

If you're a really fit mountain bike enthusiast, you might try the ride from Lee Vining to Tioga Pass, one of the most challenging you may ever encounter. It's a lot easier back down the hill to Highway 395!

As usual, the weather in this area can change rapidly. Always be prepared!

Tioga Pass Resort
(760) 647-6423
www.tiogapass.com

214

Tom's Place

Atop the Sherwood Grade, this has been a popular spot of sportsmen since the early 1920s.

Tom's Place started out in 1917, as a much needed gas station to fuel the traffic moving up from Southern California. Thomas Jefferson Yerby and his wife Hazel (stage actress Jane Grey) took over the property and build the original Tom's Place Lodge in 1924.

At time, there were few fish in the creeks. So Tom brought

trout in from hatcheries, put them in old milk cans and packed them in on horseback, stocking the lakes and creeks nearby. The original lodge burned down in 1947, and was replaced by the building that you now see.

Today hosts, Mark and Michelle Layne, are busy renovating some of the rooms and making other needed improvements to the resort. They are working hard to retain the original ambiance. For your convenience, they offer cabins, a general store, restaurant and saloon. As you stop and have dinner or a drink, look over the walls and see the countless pictures of movie stars and other famous folks that have visited over the past 80 years.

Tom's Place Resort
(760) 935-4239
www.tomsplaceresort.com

215

Twin Lakes
Double the Fun!

About 11 miles west of Bridgeport, in the Toiyabe National Forest, past the historic Hunewell Ranch, you'll find two massive lakes, both well stocked with "hungry" trout.

Nestled beneath the jagged crest of the Sawtooth Ridge, and the icy blue Matterhorn Glacier, this area is typical of the splendid beauty of the Sierra Nevada.

Naturally, the Fish and Game Department plants fish on a regular basis, as they do in most area lakes and streams.

However, this effort is enhanced by the local Twin Lakes merchants. Each season they add an extra 6,000 - 10,000 trout.

In 1987, Upper Twin Lake produced the state record brown trout, a whopping 26 pounds, 8 ounces, caught by Danny Stearman. Hey, there must be another one nearby! Fortunately, there's scrappy, pan-sized fish too.

216

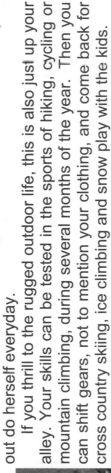

The area offers excellent fishing on Robinson, Buckeye and other adjacent streams, as well as many lakes reached by marked trails.

For those looking to just relax, or who enjoy landscape painting or photography, this is a perfect place in which to spend some time. In the autumn, gold is discovered as the leaves turn and the mountains prepare for winter. Year round, the scenic beauty is absolutely breathtaking. Mother Nature seems to try to out do herself everyday.

If you thrill to the rugged outdoor life, this is also just up your alley. Your skills can be tested in the sports of hiking, cycling or mountain climbing, during several months of the year. Then you can shift gears, not to mention your clothing, and come back for cross country skiing, ice climbing and snow play with the kids.

In the warmer months, you can water ski around the lakes, windsurf or swim and sunbath. As with any mountain area in the 7,000 foot and above range, it a good idea to pack warm clothes along with your lighter stuff for the day. Evenings around the campfire can get chilly. Always carry a jacket with you. The weather can change very rapidly.

There are many places to camp, park your RV or rent a cabin or trailer. Many of the campsites are part of a national reservation system, so you can call ahead and reserve one. Two full service resorts are on the lake to help make your stay pleasant and memorable.

217

Annett's Mono Village is situated at the end of the road on Upper Twin Lakes. It offers rental cabins, a motel and a 300 space campground. The fully stocked grocery store includes an ATM machine, propane, wood, ice, tackle and fishing licenses. The marina has a complete boat house, with boat and pontoon boat rentals. The café is considered excellent and hosts an outdoor Friday night BBQ, (Memorial Day through Labor Day). You can enjoy a cocktail at the lounge and browse the gift shop, which features clothing and assorted gift items. After a day on the lake or a long hike, use the shower and laundry facilities.

Twin Lakes Resort is the first facility you will encounter. It has cabins and an RV Park, a completed stocked general store, a laundromat and shower facilities. The marina has mooring facilities, a launch ramp, bait and tackle shop and boat rentals, including canoes and paddle boats. Good food is also available all day.

If you're interested in day rides or a pack trip, there are two saddle outfits in the area.

While here, take time to visit the old Bodie Ghost Town, the hot springs and the museum in Bridgeport.

Doc and Al's Resort offer RV and camping sites along the Robinson Creek, on the way into the Twin Lakes area.

Annetts Mono Village
(760) 932-7071
www.monovillage.com
Campground Information
(760) 932-9888
Doc and Al's Resort
(760) 932-7051
Leavitt Meadows Pack Station
(530) 495-2257
www.leavittmeadows.com
Lower Twin Lakes Resort
(800) 407-6153
www.lowertwinlakesresort.com
Virginia Lakes Pack Station
(760)937-0326
www.virginialakes.com

218

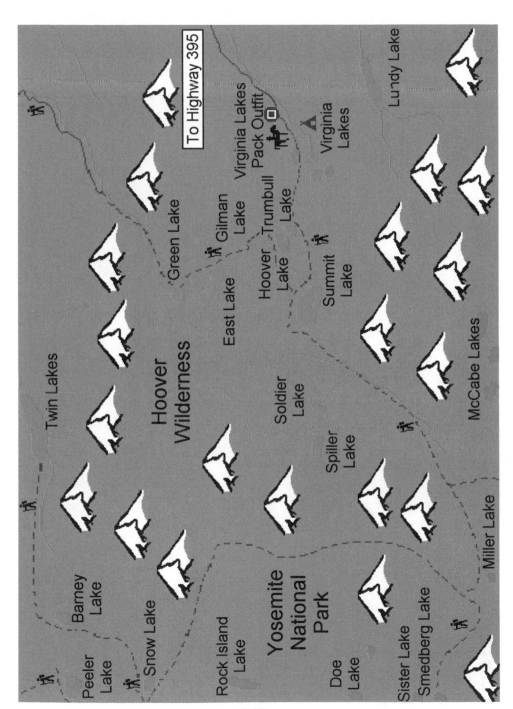

To Highway 395

Lundy Lake

Virginia Lakes Pack Outfit

Virginia Lakes

Gilman Lake

Green Lake

Hoover Lake

Trumbull Lake

East Lake

Summit Lake

Hoover Wilderness

Twin Lakes

McCabe Lakes

Soldier Lake

Spiller Lake

Miller Lake

Barney Lake

Snow Lake

Rock Island Lake

Yosemite National Park

Peeler Lake

Doe Lake

Sister Lake

Smedberg Lake

Virginia Lakes

The road to this scenic gateway to the Hoover Wilderness and parts of northern Yosemite is found off Highway 395 near Conway Summit.

It's not far and the trip is well worth the trouble. This is a wonder area for fishing, hiking, horseback riding and just plain getting away from it all.

In the Hoover Wilderness you can pick from a number of areas to visit like: Green Lake, East Lake, West Lake, Gilman Lake, Nutter Lake, Barney Lake, Peeler Lake, Crown Lake, North and South Forks of Buckeye Creek. Devils Gate and Little Walker Drainage.

There is a resort with cabins, tent camping and an RV park, with water hookups only. You can get general supplies at the store and rent a rowboat. Motors are not allowed to be used on the lake. They'll cook up a good meal for you too! There are primitive campsites around the lake.

Virginia Lakes Pack Station
(760) 937-0326 - (775) 867-2591
www.virginialakes.com
Virginia Lakes Resort
(760) 647-6484

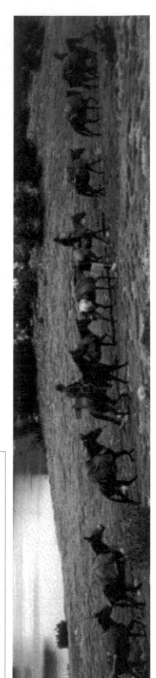

220

Walker River

Early toll roads from Carson City and Wellington followed this river. Henry Hayes lived in the Toll House Building and collected tolls from 1880 to 1915, when the c o u n t y purchased the road. Tolls were .25 for s a d d l e horses, .75 for teams and later autos.

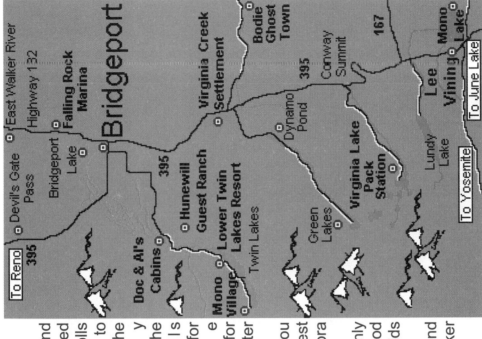

The original road was build in 1868. If you have access to a 1917 Mono National Forest map, locate the stagecoach stations at Sonora and Elbow and follow the road to Aurora.

The Walker is a challenging and suitable only for fit, athletic participants that are also good swimmers. It is a high elevation river, which adds an element of fatigue for participants.

The best time to run the Walker is June and July. There is also excellent fishing in the Walker River. Pack a lunch and enjoy yourself!

Pacific Crest National Scenic Trail

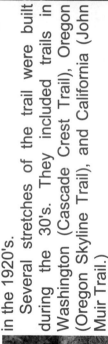

Backpacking enthusiasts worldwide come to the PCT to trek through some of the most scenic country and diverse landscapes found anywhere. The trail stretches 2,638 miles from the Mexico border to Canada. Conception and construction of the PCT began in the 1920's.

Several stretches of the trail were built during the 30's. They included trails in Washington (Cascade Crest Trail), Oregon (Oregon Skyline Trail), and California (John Muir Trail.)

The John Muir Trail begins at Happy Isles in Yosemite National Park and stretches south 212 miles to the summit of Mt. Whitney. It follows the PCT for the majority of its length. It breaks off from the PCT leading up to the summit of Mt. Whitney and in the Devils Postpile area.

Obtaining a wilderness permit to begin your trip at Mt. Whitney can be very difficult because you are competing with massive numbers of people who wish to climb Mt. Whitney. There are many access points along the trail that will shorten the trip and give you an easier time of getting a permit.

Snow conditions in the Sierra Nevada change from year to year making it difficult to predict what the conditions will be like. Snow banks are usually still present along the ridges and passes when the summer season starts. Occasional thunderstorms occur during the summer, but summer days are typically warm with nights being comfortably cool. Be prepared for rapid

changes in weather. Snow will usually cover the trails in November.

PCT foot travel on the southern part of the forest can be possible by early June, with stock travel by July 1. Higher passes may not open until as much as a month later.

The John Muir Trail is passable from July through October. Most of the trail is above 7,000 feet with some places over 13,000 feet.

Wilderness permits are needed when you plan to stay overnight in any National Park back country or Wilderness area. To obtain a permit, contact the Forest or National Park that administers your point of entry. The permit is good for one continuous trip along the John Muir Trail or PCT, from California to Washington.

Fires are restricted in certain areas along the Pacific Crest and John Muir Trails due to high fire danger or lack of dead and down wood. Know the fire restrictions before you start your trip.

Most people who travel the entire length of the John Muir Trail or any significant length of the PCT need to resupply along the way. There are

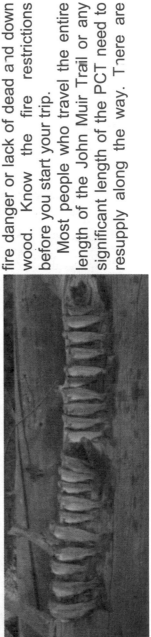

small stores just off the trail at Red's Meadow, Tuolumne Meadows, Edison Lake and Florence Lake. You can arrange with them ahead of time to obtain a resupply package. Ranger Stations or Park Service offices have details on wilderness permits, maps, guide books on the PCT or John Muir Trail, and any special regulations that are in effect. Remember stock has the right of way on trails, and pack out all you bring in.

Arrange for Supplies

There are three ways to resupply when hiking along the Trail
(1) arrange for a packer or a friend to bring food to you on the trail
(2) mail a food package to yourself at a post office near the trail,
(3) hike out to a store in a nearby town.
To mail yourself a package, address the box: YOUR NAME, GENERAL DELIVERY, P.O., State, Zip Code, HOLD UNTIL (date), The post office is legally obligated to hold a package for only ten days.

Pacific Crest Trail
www.pct.com
(559) 565-3341
Mammoth Ranger Station
(760) 924-5500
Sequoia-Kings Canyon Parks
(559) 565-3341
White Mountain Ranger Station
(760) 873-2500
Mt. Whitney Ranger Station
(760) 876-6200
Yosemite National Park
(209) 372-0200

Sequoia National Forest

Covering 1,700 square miles of scenic beauty, this forest takes its name from the giant trees that grow only in here in California's Sierra Nevada. This area is as spectacular as its trees, punctuated by majestic granite monoliths, glacier torn canyons, roaring whitewater and lush meadow lands.

Its history unfolds with Native America villages, settler's cabins, mining towns, cattle ranches, lumber camps, mineral springs and early day resorts.

Today it welcomes visitors from around the world. Statistics have shown that more foreign visitors are interested in seeing the giant sequoias visiting Disneyland, San Francisco and other tourists attraction that one might feel would generate more interest.

There are camping facilities throughout the forest, mingled with a variety of lodging accommodations. You'll find trout in almost every stream and lake. Trails leading to the beautiful backcountry are

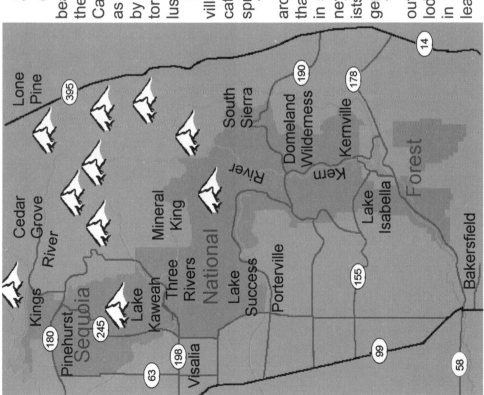

well marked. Permits for overnight stays in the wilderness are available from the Ranger Stations.

You'll want to visit Boyden Cavern, located along the Kings River, in one of the deepest canyons in North America. See the Chicago Stump, the part of the tree left from 1893, when a giant sequoia was cut down and shipped to the Columbian Exposition in Chicago, just to prove how large the trees really were. The Needles are an interesting series of massive granite rock formations rising from the North Fork of the Kern River.

Hume Lake, formed by a rare multiple arch dam in 1907, provided water for the longest lumber flume ever built. It allowed logs to travel 73 miles through the Kings Canyon to Sanger. A sawmill fire caused operations to cease in 1917. Today, the lake is a popular recreational area with boat rentals, lodging, showers, a laundry, restaurant, general store and motor vehicle fuel. Lake Isabella is one of the largest reservoirs in Southern California, covering more than 17 square miles. It too, is well visited by sailors, fishermen, campers, hikers and other outdoorsmen. All amenities are available around the lake.

Bureau of Land Management
(661) 391-6088
Camping Reservations
(877) 444-6777
www.reserveusa.com
Cannell Meadow Ranger
(760) 376-3781
Greenhorn Ranger
(760) 379-5646
Hot Springs Ranger
(661) 548-6503
Hume Lake Ranger
(559) 338-2251
Tule River Ranger
(559) 539-2607

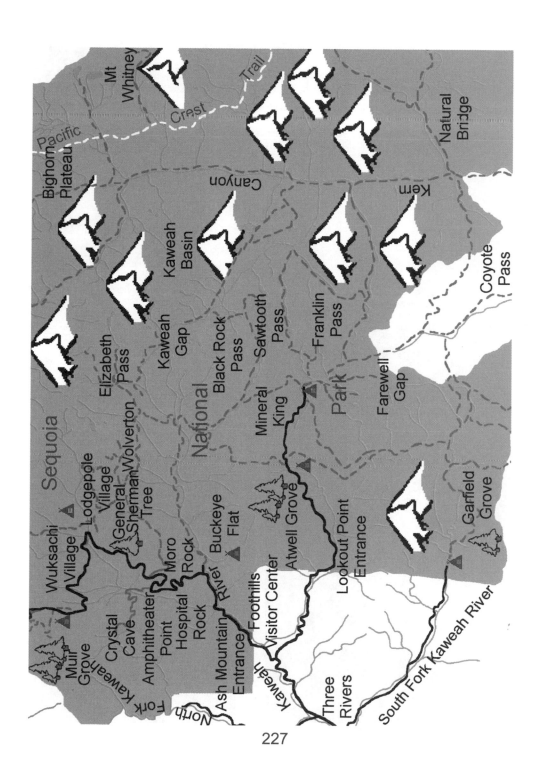

227

Sequoia National Park

Rushing waters, beautiful panoramic views, backcountry trails, abundant wildlife, an opportunity to explore caves and much more awaits you in Sequoia National Park.

Naturally, the giant sequoia is the driving force behind the naming of this magnificent park.

John Muir is quoted, "The big tree is Nature's forest masterpiece, and so far as I know, the greatest of all living things. It belongs to an ancient stock . . . and has a strange air of other days about it, a thoroughbred look inherited from the long ago—the Auld Lang Syne of Trees.

The trees Muir speaks so fondly of, are only found in the Sierra Nevada. The largest of all trees, they can tower more than 270' and reach a diameter of 35'.

There are 40 groves of them here about. Tourists come from all over the world to marvel in their shadow.

228

There are lodging accommodations, in several locations, that cater to families and singles alike, both inside the park and in the communities that surround Sequoia. You'll also find restaurants, general stores, equipment rentals and gift shops riding stables and gift shops.

Motor vehicle fuel may not be available in the park. It is suggested to enter the park with a full tank.

The park is open all year, with a variety of recreational activities available in each season. The fishing is excellent in the streams and lakes. Most are stocked regularly. Hiking trails lead you into a captivating high country. Wilderness Permits are required for all overnight stays while in the back country. You can get

them at the Rangers Station.

Places to visit inside the park include: Moro Rock, Wuksachi Village, Crystal Cave, Wolverton, the Mineral King area, Lodgepole Village, the General Sherman Tree, Hospital Rock and the Kaweah River.

The park is home to black bears, among other wildlife. You need to store your food properly to prevent bears from getting into it. Bear containers are provided in campgrounds and small ones are available from sporting good stores.

The park is a wildland recreational area. Be alert and safe as you travel. Don't swim above water falls; river currents are strong and dangerous; watch for signs of rock slides; keep your eye on the weather. Stay out of open areas during thunderstorms.

Vehicle access to Sequoia is via Highway 198 from Three Rivers and Visalia or The General's Highway from Kings Canyon National Park.

Sequoia National Park
www.nps.gov/seki
Sequoia Park Services
(559) 253-2199
www.visitsequoia.com
Camping Reservations
(877) 444-6777
www.reserveusa.com

Sierra National Forest

On the western slope of the Sierra Nevada, this forest is known for beautiful, lush, mountain scenery, a varied wealth of natural resources and tourism.

It has met the public needs for water, wood and outdoor recreation for more than a century.

Today, it is one of the most popular forests in the U.S., with its rugged terrain, the backcountry lakes, cascading water-falls, beautiful streams and hungry trout!

It encompasses over 1.3 million acres, with elevations between 900' and 13,157'. The terrain includes the oak-covered foothills, heavily

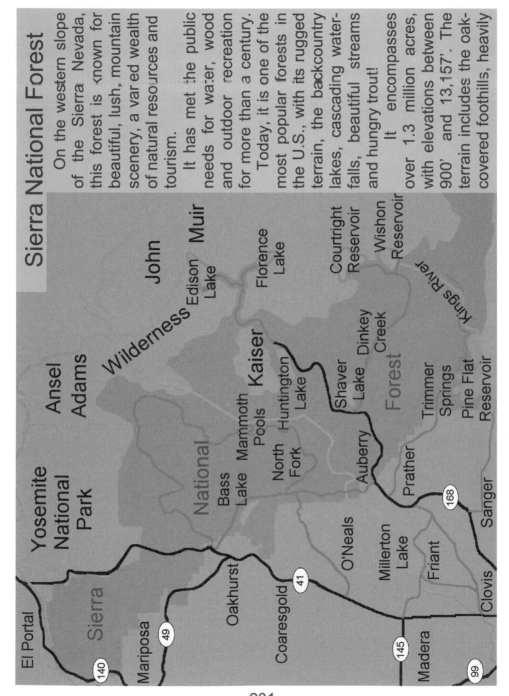

forested middle-elevation slopes and the beautiful alpine landscape of the high country. Abundant fish and wildlife, a variety of flora and fauna along with the many things to do, make this an outdoorman's paradise. The many places to visit include: Bass Lake, Dinkey Creek, El Portal near Yosemite, Fish Camp, Florence and Edison Lakes near the Pacific Crest Trail, Huntington Lake, Mono Hot Springs, Nelder Grove, McKinley Grove, Fresno Dome, Arch Rock, Redinger Lake, Mammoth Pools, Pine Flat Reservoir, Shaver Lake, Sierra Summit Ski Area, the lower King's River, Wishon and Courtright Reservoirs. More than 60 developed campgrounds await you along with many resorts, marinas and miscellaneous services.

Camping Reservations
(877) 444-6777
www.reserveusa.com
Mariposa Visitors Center
(209) 966-3638
King's River District
(559) 855-8323
Minarets Ranger District
(559) 877-2218
Pineridge Ranger District
(559) 855-5367
Yosemite Sierra Visitors Bureau
(559) 683-4636
www.go2yosemite.net

232

South Sierra

This is a vast, arid expanse of the Sierra, compared to the Central and Northern areas. Elevations range from 6,100' near Kennedy Meadows at the southern tip of the wilderness to 12,123' at Olancha Peak on the east.

The South Fork of the Kern River, a Wild and Scenic River, runs through the heart of the wilderness. Compared to other areas like Golden Trout, this wilderness gets less attention from hikers and backpackers.

Therefore, no visitor permits are required and there are no quotas on hikers and backpackers. If solitude is what you seek, try the South Sierra. Bring water, food, warm clothing, and a tent if you intend to stay overnight. There are no facilities in this wilderness.

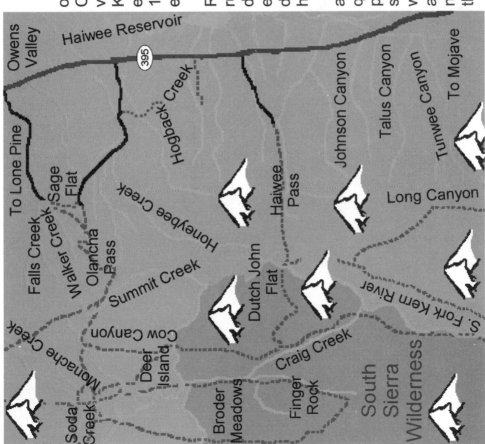

Don't get the idea that this place is untouched by humans, though. According to archaeologists, folks have been here for at least 6,000 years. Though the wilderness has not been completely surveyed, scientists have found bedrock mortars and obsidian objects that Native Americans used. It is believed that Owens Valley Paiute and the Panamin Shoshone once lived in these parts. The Sierra Nevada red fox , the marten and the pine fisher are found in this area. The wolverine was last seen in this vicinity during the 1950s.

The mule deer is the most frequently seen large animal, most noticeable in the summer after the birth of fawns. The deer's biggest enemy is the mountain lion , which hikers don't usually see because it is so secretive.

Access to the area is from Lone Pine, 28 miles south on 395 to Sage Flat Road , turn right. Drive about 5 miles west on Sage Flat Road to the trailhead for Olancha Pass or go 4 miles south of the Sage Flat Road turnoff on Highway 395 to Haiwee Canyon Road and turning right, about 2.8 miles to trailhead parking and hike into the wilderness. Activities: Hiking, backpacking, picnicking, photography, and fishing. Open year-round, but the best hiking season is May through Oct.

Mount Whitney Ranger Station
(760) 876 6200

Stanislaus Forest

Okay, where can you fish in over 800 miles of rivers and streams, stay in a campground, or hike into the backcountry to find solitude and pristine conditions, swim near a sandy beach, raft the breathtaking Tuolumne River, or canoe on one of the many gorgeous lakes, ride a horse, hop aboard a mountain bike and drive around on a snowmobile?

Well, here's the answer: Stanislaus National Forest! Consisting of 898,000 acres of recreational and natural resource production, this beautiful area beckons you.

Various degrees of accessibility exist at many of the recreation sites for Persons with Disabilities. Permits are required for gathering firewood, gathering mushrooms, rafting, hunting, fishing, venturing into the backcountry and livestock

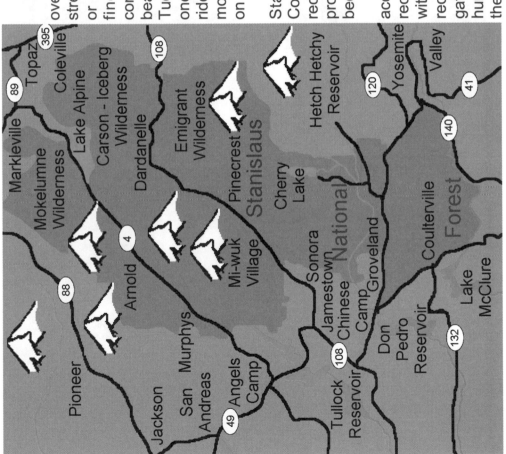

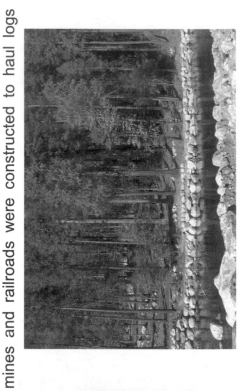

grazing. They can be obtained from a Ranger Station.

The name Stanislaus comes from Indian leader, Estanislao. This was once the home of the Me-Wuk Indians. They lived in permanent villages and temporary camps near springs or along small creeks. They raised a variety of edible plants and traded with other Indians of the Mono Lake area for obsidian, pine nuts and other items. A replica of a Me-Wuk village is open to visitors, near Pinecrest.

During the gold rush era, the place was overrun with miners, gamblers, cattlemen, homesteaders, dam builders, loggers and others. Ditches were built to bring water to the mines and railroads were constructed to haul logs

236

Aspen Meadow Pack Station
(209) 965-3402
Calaveras Ranger District
(209) 795-1381
Camping Reservations
(877) 444-6777
www.reserveusa.com
Groveland Ranger District
(209) 962-7825
Kennedy Meadow Pack Station
(209) 965-3900
www.kennedymeadows.com
Summit Ranger District
(209) 965-3434

out of the woods.

The river is very popular with rafters. Check with the rangers to determine the best access points if you have your own equipment.

There are several excellent and well trained outfitters that will help plan a day or extended trip for you.

It's best to stay overnight in the area when you are planning a trip on the river, because the action usually starts early in the morning.

Winter months feature snow play areas, cross country and alpine skiing. A variety of lodging is available from primitive camping to hotels and resorts. All services are available in the area.

Toiyabe National Forest

This has the distinction of being the country's largest National Forest outside of Alaska, with a part in California and the balance in Nevada, with a net of about 4 million acres.

There are three wilderness areas within the Sierra Nevada portion: the Hoover, Mokelumne and Carson-Iceberg.

The climate differs from one part of the Forest to the other. Some areas are arid and desert-like. Others include alpine lakes and snow capped ridges.

The wide plains of the interrange valleys provide you with a striking contrast to the overall ruggedness of the high, rocky mountain ranges above.

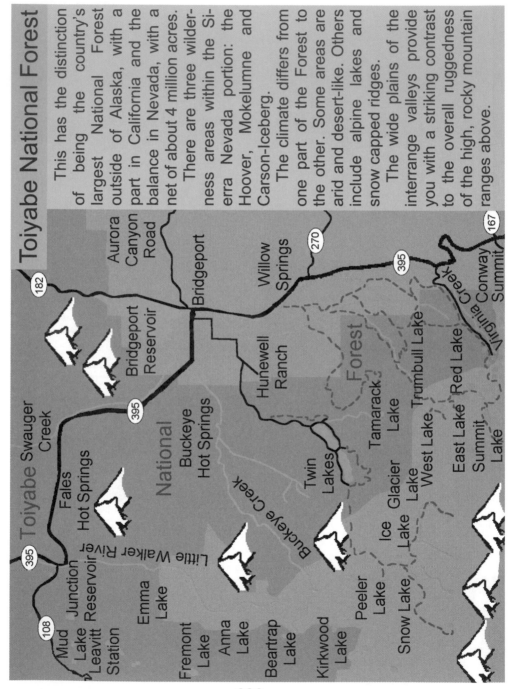

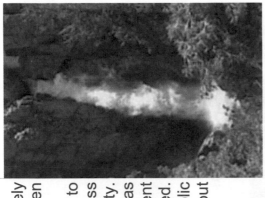

Most of its reaches can be safely traversed by experienced horsemen or backpackers.

One should have the ability to read topographic maps, a compass and be well versed in outdoor safety. At the same time, there are areas where technical climbing equipment and techniques must be employed.

There are 35 developed public campgrounds in the area with about 900 family and group sites.

Other developed facilities that are available here include eight picnic grounds, multiple observation sites, trailheads, snowplay areas, cross-country skiing and two ski resorts.

Naturally, like any forest area, you can spend your time with camping, hiking, fishing, hunting, skiing, canoeing, horseback riding

and sightseeing.

The Toiyabe provides over 1,100 miles of trails for hiking, backpacking and horseback riding. The forest also offers over 1,600 miles of recreation roads for travel and viewing scenery.

There are numerous small caves scattered across the Toiyabe. Be careful when you explore them.

The most common of the larger wildlife species of the Toiyabe is the mule deer. The black bear, mountain lion and bobcat also inhabit the area, and though seldom seen, there are desert bighorn sheep. Wild burros and horses are found throughout the Excelsior Range of the Bridgeport area. Innumerable small mammals and reptiles are found throughout the territory.

You'll also encounter lots of birds, including grouse, mountain quail, red-tailed hawks, the golden and bald eagles in this beautiful region. Bring your camera!

240

Tulare County

Created in 1852, and now covering 4,935 square miles, or 3,158,400 acres, this is one of the state's largest counties. It has undergone a number of changes and the boundaries finally settled upon in 1893.

It has a massive coverage of scenic mountains covering nearly half of its area on the east side, with the balance of its expanse being a level and fertile plain.

A variety of facilities are available for overnight stays. You can choose from hotels, motels, bed & breakfast inns, resorts and over a thousand campsites.

There are several fine golf courses throughout the area for your enjoyment. Most are very challenging!

Every sunrise brings a new day to enjoy your visit. This is a vacation wonderland where there is literally something for everyone in the family to enjoy. In the spring, the winter runoff helps swell the rivers and the whitewater adventures begin.

Be it a raft, kayak or old inner tube, it's a thrill to ride the rapids. There are several outfitters to help you enjoy the experience. Fishing is a year round passtime, with bass, blue gill, catfish and crappie waiting to give you a fight until the trout season. Naturally, the mountain lakes and streams are stocked with hungry fish.

Sailors and houseboat enthusiasts have two great lakes to visit: Lake Kaweah and Lake Success. Each has camping facilities and services to help make your stay successful.

Backpackers, day hikers and horseback riders have scores of trails to explore. The giant sequoias are always an awe inspiring sight. There are 40 groves of these huge trees in the Sierra Nevada. Many are right here in the county!

Camping Reservations
(877) 444-6777
www.reserveusa.com
Sequoia Regional Visitors Council
(559) 734-5876 ext. 15
www.sequoia-regional-visitors-council.com
Tulare County
www.co.tulare.ca.us
Visitors Bureau
(559) 734-5876 ext. 15
www.visaliatourism.com

Crystal Cave

In 1918, two Sequoia Park trail construction employees were fishing along Cascade Creek and quite accidentally discovered the cave.

Former Park Superintendent and caving enthusiast, Walter Fry, led the first exploration party into the cave shortly thereafter.

He remembers: "It is in this cave that nature has lavishly traced her design in decorative glory. Throughout the entire cave the stalactite formations are rich and wonderfully varied in size, form and color. In some of the chambers the ceiling is a mass of stalactites, some very large, others tapering down to needle points. Others drop down from the roof (in) great folds of massive draperies, while yet others are great fluted columns of stalagmites of surpassing symmetry and beauty."

Crystal Cave is off the Generals Highway, between the Ash Mountain entry and Giant Forest. Drive down the scenic, winding, paved road to the cave parking lot. Hike down the half-mile trail along beautiful Cascade Creek. You'll be met by a guide. No buses, trailers, or vehicles over 20 feet long are permitted on Crystal Cave Road. Tickets are only scld at the Foothills and Lodgepole Visitor Centers. Allow at least 1 ½ hours to arrive at the cave. The temperature in the cave is a constant 48 degrees F. Sweaters or jackets are recommended. No strollers or backpacks allowed in the cave.

Sequoia Natural History Association
(559) 565-3759
www.sequoiahistory.crg

Eagle Mountain Casino

While in the Porterville-Springville area, visit the casino and try your luck. You will be treated to great gaming opportunities and a full schedule of entertainment events. Sit down to a game of Blackjack. Enjoy the latest in Vegas-style slots on one of the 700 exciting machines or play bingo in their 450-seat hall.

When you get hungry you have choices. If you're not too hungry, you can simply have a snack in the main casino or bingo hall.

However, if a full meal is more to your liking, head over to the High Stakes Restaurant, which features a relaxing atmosphere and great food at very economical prices. Folks drive long distances just to enjoy the casino's fabulous buffets.

The Eagle Mountain Casino is off Highway 190, east of Porterville, on the Tule River Indian Reservation. If you're staying in Porterville, Bakersfield, Visalia, Exeter, Lindsay or Springville, you can catch a ride to the casino on the regularly scheduled Eagle Express. Contact the casino for departure details.

The drive out to the casino is very beautiful. Take time to visit the Painted Rock Ancient Heritage Site.

Eagle Mountain Casino
(800) 903-3353
(559) 788-6220
Eagle's Nest Resort
(559) 784-3948

Lake Kaweah

Lake Kaweah is fed by a river of the same name, originating in the midst of Sequoia National Park. It has one of the shortest drainages in the country from its headwaters at 12,000 feet to the lake.

Like its neighbors the Kings, Tule and Kern, it never sees the Pacific Ocean. Whatever water that doesn't get consumed by irrigation ends up in Tulare Lake.

Long age, Yokuts, Wukchumne and Kaweah Indians roamed along this river. The Spanish were the first Europeans to enter the area, over two centuries ago. Settlers started to arrive fifty years later as news of gold fueled a huge western migration.

Today, it's a popular vacation paradise. Horse Creek has 80 campsites with tables and fire rings, flush toilets, showers, a playground and a RV dump station. Campfire programs are presented at the Horse Creek Amphitheater on Saturday nights from Memorial Day weekend through Labor Day. The lake offers water-skiing, sailing, houseboating and swimming.

Launch ramps are located in the Kaweah and Lemon Hill recreation areas. The marina at Lemon Hill offers boating and camping supplies, fishing tackle, a snack bar, boat rentals, fuel and fishing licenses. Picnic spots are numerable around the lake. Swimming is permitted, except at posted areas near boat ramps and the dam's intake structure. Along the mile hiking trail between Slick Rock and Cobble Knoll you can enjoy bird-watching and wildflowers.

Lake Kaweah Information
(559) 597-2301
Tulare County Boat Patrol
(559) 597-2437

245

Lake Success

Success Lake on the Tule River, eight miles east of Porterville, is a multipurpose facility, built for flood control and irrigation. It also provides waters for fish, wildlife and outdoor activities.

Camping is available in the Tule Recreation Area. No hookups are available, but each site has a paved parking spur, picnic table and grill. All are close to restrooms with showers. An RV dump station is located nearby. All campsites are available on a first-come first served basis. The lake offers fishing, water skiing, houseboating and sailing.

Two launch ramps are located in the Tule Recreation Area. One is in the Rocky Hill Area. The marina, in the Tule Recreation Area, has boating supplies, rentals and fuel.

Picnic areas can be found in three recreation areas. Some have tables, shelters, grills and playgrounds. Success Lake is full of

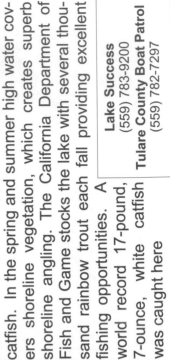

black bass, white crappie, blue gill and channel catfish. In the spring and summer high water covers shoreline vegetation, which creates superb shoreline angling. The California Department of Fish and Game stocks the lake with several thousand rainbow trout each fall providing excellent fishing opportunities. A world record 17-pound, 7-ounce, white catfish was caught here

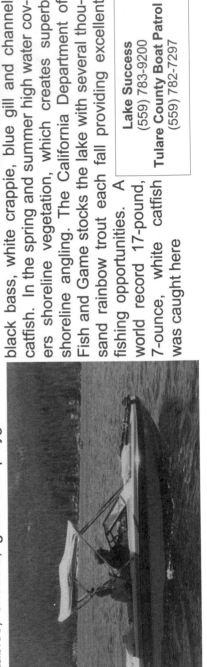

246

Porterville

Located, on 190, east of Highway 99, between Visalia and Delano, Porterville is another gateway to the Sierra.

From here you can choose the recreational area of Lake Success, head further east into the Golden Trout Wilderness or over to Sequoia National Park.

There are a number of fine facilities for lodging and dining. Vacationers can also find groceries, sporting goods, boating supplies and all major services .

You can visit the Porterville Historical Museum housed in the old 1913 Southern Pacific passenger station at 257 North D Street. You'll see vignettes of a dentist's office, a crug store and an attorney's office, as well as china, furniture, glassware and American Indian artifacts, including baskets created by the Yokuts. It's usually open Thursday through Saturday.

Another local site of interest is the Zalud House, at 393 N Hockett. It was built in 1891, and is remarkable for having been lived in exclusively by the Zalud family until 1970. Mr. Zalud was a rancher and saloon owner. The saloon was closed in the 1920s, due to prohibition. You can take a tour of the property. It is now furnished entirely with original Zalud family possessions just as it was when the family was in residence. Open to the public Wednesday through Sunday.

Porterville Chamber
(559) 784-7502
Porterville Historical Museum
(559) 784-2C53
Zalud House
(559) 782-7548

247

Springville

This rural foothill community is a popular jump off point to the new Giant Sequoia Monument and the Ponderosa recreational area. There are a variety of places to spend the night, including campgrounds, resorts and lodging facilities.

See the giant trees, camp, fish, hike or take a horseback ride in the beautiful backcountry of the Sierra.

Springville sponsors several family fun events each year. A springtime PRCA Rodeo draws contestants from around the country, and don't count out the local cowboys either. They're fierce competitors.

Each October, the Apple Festival, a family-oriented event, attracts more than 30,000 visitors. Hey, a pie eating contest always draws a crowd! Browse through the arts and crafts displays, try the delicious food and let the kids enjoy the clowns and all the other fun. Bring your square dancing duds and kick the straw around the floor!

This is an area popular with mountain bikers, and for golfers, there's a beautiful 18-hole course designed around a wildlife sanctuary along the Middle Fork of the Tule River.

Camp Nelson Lodge
(559) 542-0904
www.campnelsonlodge.com
Cedar Slope Inn
(559) 542-2319
Friends of the Tule River
(559) 539-8401
Mountain Top B&B
(559) 542-2639 (888) 867-4784
River Island Country Club
(559) 784-9425
Ponderosa Lodge
(559) 542-2579
Slate Mountain Resort
(559) 542-1900
Springville Chamber
(559) 539-2312
www.springville.ca.us
Tule River Ranger Station
(559) 539-2607

Three Rivers

Located on the Kaweah River at the junction of its tributaries, this is a major entry point to Sequoia National Park. Before the mid-1850's the area was populated by the Yokut Indians. They found the area, with native oak trees, plants, fish and small animals, to be a land of plenty.

In 1856 Hale Tharp, the first documented white man in the area, settled on the river bottom, raising cattle and hogs. By the 1870's many other farmers came and agreed this was ideal place to raise livestock. Additionally, orchards of fruit and citrus trees were planted and thrived in the area. A short lived boom was caused when silver ore veins were found in the Mineral King Valley. Many of the former miners settled here.

Recreational activities fund this town, with boating at the lake to hiking along the forks of the river and white water rafting thrills in the spring and early summer. Try fishing the lake and rivers or perhaps the catfish farm. If golf is your game, then enjoy nine holes along the Kaweah River.

Local Artisans offer art and sculpture as they present their inspirations at the Red Bud Festival held each spring. Lodging is available whether your interest is a charming Bed & Breakfast, a cabin or an outstanding motels, they're all here.

249

Visalia

Nestled at the base of the magnificent Sierra, this a major gateway to Sequoia and Kings Canyon National Parks. These beautiful recreational areas offer some of the most diverse and dramatic landscapes in North America.

The summit of Mount Whitney, at 14,494', is on Sequoia's eastern boundary. It is the tallest peak in the continental United States.

The majestic giant sequoia trees can reach heights of 720 feet. There are panoramas of lakes, ev-

ergreens, meadows and wildlife throughout the forest.

All this, just an hour's drive. Literally in the back yard are water skiing, snow skiing, fishing, backpacking, boating, kayaking, white water rafting, mountain biking, hiking, camping and exploring caverns.

A variety of lodging and dining facilities, plus complete services are available in town.

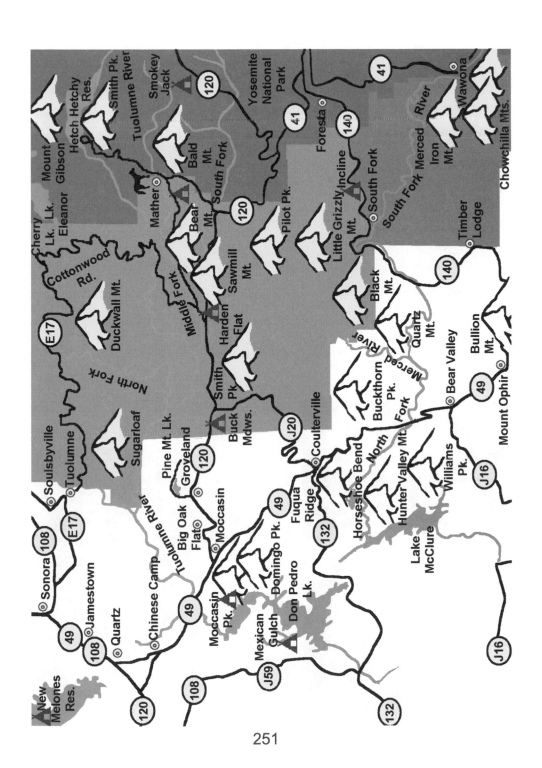

251

Tuolumne County

Referred to as "the great unfenced" by those who know it best, Tuolumne County has it all. You can explore remote mountain steams, lakes and reservoirs.

The Stanislaus National Forest features 811 miles of rivers and steams with 18 species of fish. Take a pack trip with horseback guides to the Emigrant Wilderness.

Since this is the heart of gold country, you can try your hand at gold mining or panning. You'll see evidence of extensive hydraulic mining along Highway 49. Tour the Historic Site of Columbia, a famous gold mining community.

Consider a whitewater adventure camping trip. Take a houseboat vacation. Ride the old train at Jamestown. Attend the music festival at Strawberry. Glide down the slopes at Doge Ridge. Check out life along Highways 120, 108 and 49.

There are plenty of accommodations for you and your family. Choose from hotels, motels, B&B inns, groomed campgrounds or back country primitive sites. All necessary items for a successful vacation are available to you as you travel thru this beautiful section of the Sierra Nevada!

Chinese Camp

In 1849, 35 Cantonese miners arrived at Camp Salvado to find gold. Where and why they came is a mystery. Some say a ship's captain left his vessel in San Francisco Bay and brought his crew with him to the mines.

Others say they were employed by English speculators to search for gold. No matter what story is true, they found gold and the claims were rich. Soon, white miners arrived and pushing the Chinese out.

However the miners at Camp Washington, accepted the outcast Chinese miners without problems. The lack of water in the area, needed for working the placers, may be one reason why the Chinese were able to establish a successful camp without much interference from the white miners. Being more patient and industrious than their American counterparts, the Chinese miners were willing to work harder and for less return than the white miners, often making good wages on claims abandoned by other miners.

When the post office was established on April 18 of 1854, the town was named Chinese Camp. The town's location made Chinese Camp the center of transportation for a large area, several stage and freight lines made regular daily stops here on their way to other points. During the mid-1850's, an estimated three to five thousand inhabitants lived in the area and the camp boasted several stores, hotels, blacksmiths, a church, a bank, a Wells Fargo office, a Masonic Lodge, and the Sons of Temperance. Four of the famous Chinese "Six Companies" had their agents in town. The placer mines of this area are credited with producing $2.5 million in gold.

Chinese Camp
www.malakoft.com

253

Columbia

In early 1850, newly arrived miners picked nuggets right off the grounds in the surrounding foothills. In just a few days they had collected nearly 30 pounds.

Naturally the word of this spread through the California gold camps and miners flocked to the area. Within a month, the town population grew to over 5,000, mostly prospectors!

Using the new method

of placer mining, the miners quickly created one of the highest yielding gold fields in the state.

Today, much of the town looks much like it did back then. It's a great place to take the family for a tour. You can stay at the old City Hotel, still a fine facility with old time ambiance and fantastic restaurant.

On weekends you might be lucky enough to catch some local musicians with a love for bluegrass music playing at the local saloon.

254

Let the kids enjoy an exciting gold panning tour at the beautiful Marble Quarry Park. During the tour they are taught the techniques of gold panning while hearing about gold's interesting history, uses and properties. They'll experience the hands-on thrill of the '49ers as they swirl their pan for gold!

Head on over to the Wells Fargo Building on Main Street and arrange to ride the old 1856 horse-drawn stage. You can also take a horseback ride or pony rides through the historic mining country surrounding the old town.

There are antique shops, an old fashioned ice cream parlor and gift shops to browse. You'll find several shady picnic spots if you want to take a lunch with you. Of course, there are many places to arrange for a good meal or favorite libation!

Ask about the wine tasting facilities in town. Columbia is a State Park and open all year.

Dodge Ridge

Just thirty miles east of Sonora, on Highway 108, you'll find a complete winter sports recreational paradise. Dodge Ridge features downhill skiing, snow-boarding, cross-country skiing and snowshoe trails. There are at least 60 runs, 12 ski lifts and a vertical drop of 1600'. That's not all.

There are also a 11 km groomed track, two restaurants, adult and children ski school programs and rentals. Full services and complete lodging are available.

They recently added Boulder Creek Canyon and the response has been overwhelming. It features a new quad, spectacular vistas and a world class skiing experience. The two intermediate routes down the Canyon are Graceland and Creekside. The first is the gentler of the two, located on the skier's left of the top lift terminal. Creekside to Boulder Over is accessed from the skier's right of the lift.

The remainder of the runs are all very challenging and provide Dodge Ridge's steepest (Six Shooter) and best views (Sure Shot). Sunrise and Sundown are home to the Santa Cruz Snowpark and the Santa Cruz Halfpipe, popular with snowboarders and skiers as the biggest parks at Dodge Ridge.

Dodge Ridge Ski Area
(209) 965-3474
www.dodgeridge.com
Mi Wuk Village Inn & Resort
(209) 586-3031
www.miwukvillageinn.com
Pinecrest Chalet
(209) 965-3276
www.pinecrestchalet.com
Pinecrest Lake Resort
(209) 965-3411
www.pinecrestlakeresort.com
Shadow Ridge Vacation Rentals
(800) 382-0334
(209) 586-0334
www.shadowridge.com

Groveland

Located on Highway 120 and 26 miles from the Yosemite Park entrance, the historic community of Groveland is the most convenient gateway for tourists coming from the San Francisco Bay area, Sacramento or Stockton and Modesto.

Groveland is also home to the infamous Iron Door Saloon, said to be the oldest continuously operating saloon in California.

Gold, water and Yosemite are all responsible for creating this natural stopping off point on Highway 120. The story of Groveland's development is quite interesting. As with most towns in the area, it all started with gold! James Savage discovered gold here in 1848. Savage's Diggins became Garrotte in 1850 and was a boom town. By the 1870's, it was transformed from dozens of bars and bordellos to a quiet place with cattle ranches and a trickle of tourists taking the new Big Oak Flat Road to Yosemite.

Groveland experienced a second gold rush with the advent of deep shaft mines and milling operations.

It was over by 1914, but a third rush began with the congressional approval to build the Hetch Hetchy Project.

Evergreen Lodge
(209) 379-2606 (800) 935-6343
www.evergreenlodge.com
Groveland Hotel
(209) 962-4000
(800) 273-3314
www.groveland.com
Highway 120 Chamber
(209) 962-0429
www.groveland.org
Historic Iron Door Saloon
(209) 962-8904

Hotel Charlotte
(209) 962-6455 (209) 962-7872
Mather Saddle and Pack Station
(209) 379-2334
Winter (209) 847-5753
www.mathersaddleandpackstation.com
Pine Mountain Lake
(209) 962-8638
www.pinemountainlake.com
Vintage Gold Wine Bar & Bottle Shop
(209) 962-4600
www.vintagegold.com

Jamestown

The site of the first gold find in Tuolumne County, Jamestown has always been a popular place to hang around. It was first known as Woods Crossing, but soon renamed Jamestown in honor of Col. James. The town folks loved him. He wined and dined them before falling on bad times and disappearing with their money.

This is the home of the Sierra Railroad Museum. It's close to Lake Tulloch and lots of water sport activities. You can try gold panning and learn about the history of the miners.

There's great food and a variety of excellent lodging, including hotels, motels, B&B inns and nearby campgrounds. As usual, be sure to bring your camera!

Gold Prospecting Expeditions
(209) 984-4653 (800) 596-0009
www.goldprospecting.com
Historic National Hotel
(209) 984-3446 (800) 894-3446
www.national-hotel.com
Jamestown Hotel
(209) 984-3902 (800) 205-4901
jamestownhotel.com
Lake Tulloch RV & Marina
(209) 881-0107 (800) 894-CAMP
www.laketullochcampground.com
Railtown 1897 State Historic Park
(209) 984-3953 (209) 984-1600
www.railtown1897.org

Lake Don Pedro

If you want to get away from the boating crowds, then give this waterway a try. There are over 160 miles of shoreline to explore.

The camping facility offers 550 campsites featuring full RV hookups. Each site has a table, food locker and barbecue.

Enjoy boating, fishing, swimming, water skiing and houseboating, or ride around on a jet ski or try windsurfing. It's not unusual for fishermen to hook 12-pound bass!

There are two marinas to help make sure your visit is a success. You can rent boats, get needed repairs, have a snack or get fuel. Fleming Meadows has a swimming lagoon along with its picnic facility. It is a two-acre water play area with a nice sandy beach and a maximum depth of six feet. Always swim with a partner.

The spring is very pleasant, the summers can be very hot and the winters are mild.

Don Pedro Camping
(209) 852-2396
www.donpedrolake.com
West Side Marina
(209) 852-2369
East Side Marina
(209) 989-2206
Moccasin Point Marina
(209) 989-2206
(800) 255-5561

Long Barn

Nestled in the pines along Highway 108, this year round resort has lots to offer visitors. In the winter, you can ice skate at Long Barn Lodge. The Dodge Ridge Ski Resort, offering excellent winter sports, is 15 minutes away. The Leland High Sierra snow play area offers sledding and tubing. It's just a few minutes away too. If you want some variety in your skiing you can try Bear Valley and Badger Pass. Both are within a reasonable driving distance.

During the summer, you can head up to Pinecrest Lake, where you can swim, take a paddle boat ride or just relax on the beach.

Anytime of the year, a short drive will take you to three of California's historic Gold Rush communities: Sonora, Jamestown and Columbia. Each offers wonderful photo opportunities, unique stores, great restaurants and much more. At Jamestown you can ride an authentic steam engine train!

There are excellent accommodations in Long Barn. One has the extra amenities of barbeque pits, picnic tables, horseshoe pits, a volleyball court and game room for the kids.

260

New Melones Lake

Located between the old mining towns of Sonora and Angels Camp on Highway 49, New Melones is nestled in the Sierra foothills at 1100'. There are a variety of recreational opportunities awaiting you.

The Gloryhole and Tuttletown Recreation Areas have a total of five campgrounds, with 305 campsites, 5 day-use areas, 30 miles of hiking and biking trails, a fish cleaning station, a swimming beach, three boat launch ramps, a full service marina and a store complete with fuel and boat rentals.

Campgrounds all have back in, pull through, and walk-in tent sites, complete with fire rings, picnic tables, shade trees, shared water, flush toilets and showers.

New Melones Recreation Office
(209) 536-9094
www.recreation.gov
New Melones Lake Marina
(209) 785-3300
www.houseboats.com
Park Ranger
(209) 536-9094

Pinecrest Lake

Fun for all seasons would best describe the Pinecrest Lake area. In the spring, summer and fall, you can try your skill at fishing in the nearby lakes and streams. They are stocked weekly. You can also hike or ride your mountain bike along the many back country trails. For those so inclined, you may play tennis on a championship court.

The lake is a wonderful place to take an afternoon swim, enjoy a

number of water sports or just relax on the sandy beach. You can rent fishing boat and motor, a paddle boat or try out a single or double kayak.

During the winter, the snow flies and that's good news for folks that enjoy alpine and cross country skiing. Dodge Ridge Ski Resort is only minutes away. The Leland High Sierra Snow Play area is also a short drive. It offers tube and saucer rentals, a snack bar, games and a warm, wood burning stove!

You can check with the Summit Ranger District Office for more on some of the best opportunities in Tuolumne County. If you plan to stay overnight in the forest, you will most likely need a Wilderness permit. The rangers can provide them.

Pinecrest Chalet
(209) 965-3276
www.pinecrestchalet.com
Pinecrest Lake Lodge
(209) 965-3411
www.pinecrestlakeresort.com
Pinecrest Lake Marina
(209) 965-3333
Summit Ranger District
(209) 965-3434 Highway 108
www.r5.fs.fed.us/stanislaus/

Sonora

Some of the most interesting effects of hydraulic mining can be seen in the surrounding area. The town is rich in mining and ranching history.

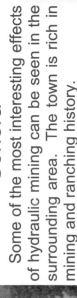

263

Strawberry

High in California's Sierra Nevada mountains, nestled among tall pines, the little community of Strawberry welcomes you. It is known as "the Gateway to the Emigrant Wilderness."

It is also known as the host of a nationally known annual musical festival, featuring bluegrass artists. Thousands of music lovers descend upon the area each year for the event.

On Highway 108, the town is close to some fantastic fly fishing on the Stanislaus River. Lots of trout call the surrounding waters home. Catch them, and you can call them "dinner"! Pinecrest Lake is minutes away. Rent a boat, kayak or paddle boat or just relax in the sun.

Lots of hiking trails are near. If you want to explore the back country on horseback, you just take a short drive. You can take an hourly ride or have them plan an extended pack trip for you.

For winter adventures, you can cross-country ski right outside the door, or you go on up the road to the Dodge Ridge Ski Area.

Kennedy Meadows Pack Station
(209) 965-3900
www.kennedymeadows.com
Leland High Sierra Snow Play
(209) 965-4719
Strawberry Inn
(209) 965-3662 (800) 965-3662.
www.strawberryinn.com

264

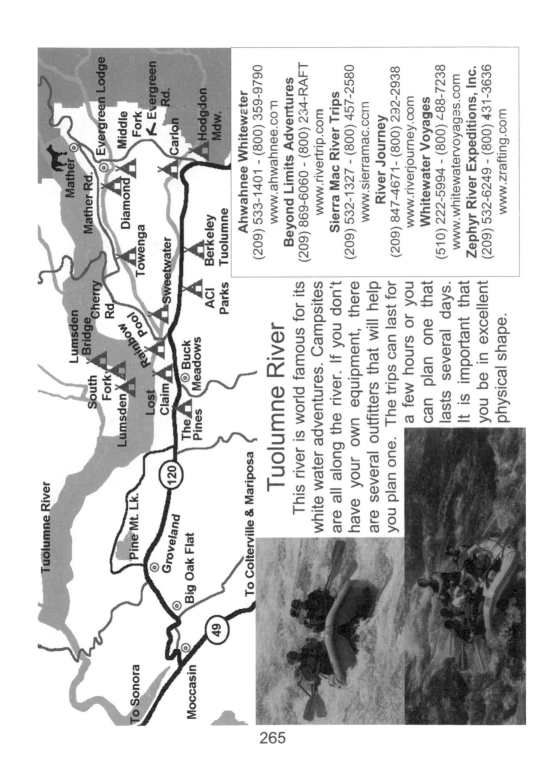

Tuolumne River

This river is world famous for its white water adventures. Campsites are all along the river. If you don't have your own equipment, there are several outfitters that will help you plan one. The trips can last for a few hours or you can plan one that lasts several days. It is important that you be in excellent physical shape.

Ahwahnee Whitewater
(209) 533-1401 - (800) 359-9790
www.ahwahnee.com

Beyond Limits Adventures
(209) 869-6060 - (800) 234-RAFT
www.rivertrip.com

Sierra Mac River Trips
(209) 532-1327 - (800) 457-2580
www.sierramac.ccm

River Journey
(209) 847-4671- (800) 232-2938
www.riverjourney.com

Whitewater Voyages
(510) 222-5994 - (800) 488-7238
www.whitewatervoyages.com

Zephyr River Expeditions, Inc.
(209) 532-6249 - (800) 431-3636
www.zrafting.com

Twain Harte

Another of the many pleasant small communities along Highway 108, this one has a golf course and tennis courts! There are few places where you can catch your limit in the morning and play a round of golf or a few sets of tennis in the afternoon.

Perhaps autumn is the most interesting season. Hunters roam the forests. The Aspen groves turn mute gold and bright red. The orange mountain oaks paint the slopes. It is just another stroke of Mother Nature's brush on the canvas called the Sierra Nevada.

Excellent lodging, fine dining, art galleries and antique shops are here for your pleasure.

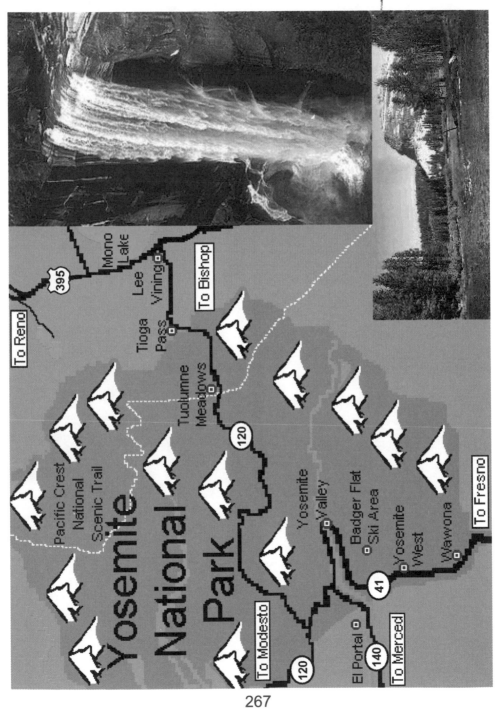

Yosemite National Park

As you've most likely heard, this is one of the most unique arenas in which Mother Nature has ever worked her magic! It truly must be seen to be appreciated. The maps on the next two pages will help you to navigate this beautiful national treasure.

Being a major recreational attraction, it naturally offers all the amenities you would expect. In the summer, the two most popular activities are hiking and mountain biking. You can carry your fishing pole with you while enjoying both! Horseback riding, swimming and rock climbing are well represented too!

In the winter, cross country skiing, ice climbing, ice skating, snowshoe hiking and sightseeing top the list.

Be sure to bring you camera whenever you come to the park. It's one of the most photographed places in the entire world.

Come play in it! Come photographic it. Come experience it. Be aware that Highway 120 is closed from Crane Flat to east of the Tioga Entrance in the winter.

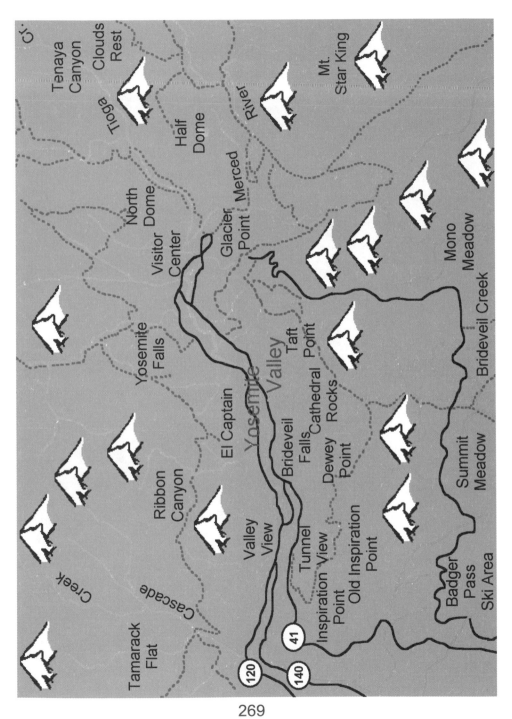

Cr.

Tenaya Canyon

Clouds Rest

Tioga

Half Dome

North Dome

Visitor Center

Merced River

Glacier Point

Mt. Star King

Mono Meadow

Yosemite Falls

El Captain

Yosemite Valley

Taft Point

Cathedral Rocks

Bridevil Creek

Brideveil Falls

Dewey Point

Summit Meadow

Ribbon Canyon

Valley View

Tunnel View

Inspiration Point

Old Inspiration Point

Badger Pass Ski Area

Cascade

Creek

Tamarack Flat

41

120

140

269

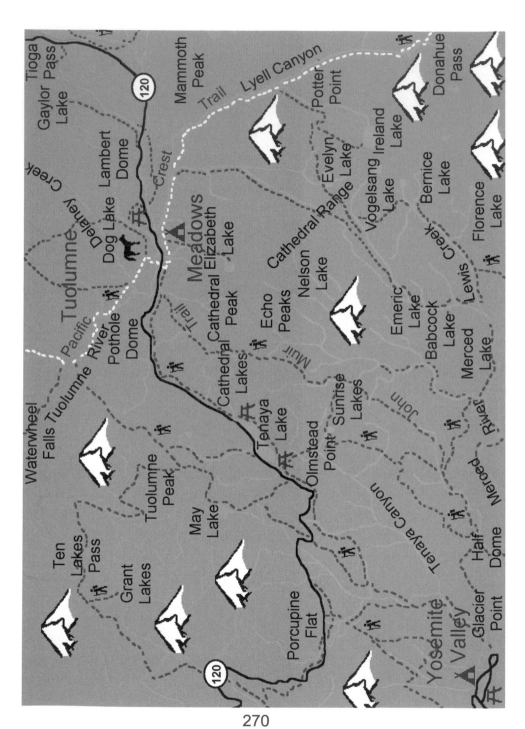

Tips for Traveling Safely

Fire in the forest.

Campfires are romantic, useful for cooking or keeping warm and very dangerous. When building campfires, use an existing fire ring at least 100 feet from water and trails. Only select dead and down wood. Standing dead trees are homes for many forest animals, don't pull them down. Use good sense. Keep your fire small, never leave it unattended and make sure it is out *cold* when you leave.

Trail Manners

Traveling in the forest is a tranquil and yet exhilarating experience all at the same time. Ettiquette is important. Leave no trace of your being there! Take all your trash out with you. Stay on existing trails. Walking on the shoulder of a wet or muddy trail causes double or triple rutting. Cutting switchbacks and short cutting the trail causes serious erosion that is expensive to repair. When you travel off the trail, stay well off it. Stock users have the right-of-way on trails. For everyone's safety, quietly stand on the downhill side of the trail as the horses, mules and llamas pass. Don't attempt to touch the animals. Startling a string of pack animals can be very dangerous.

Wilderness Hygiene

Remember that all soaps pollute, even those claiming to be biodegradable. Carry water to your camp for cooking and washing. Protect the streams, creeks, springs and lakes by keeping wash water, food scraps, fish entrails and all other wastes at least 100 feet from water. Bury all human waste six to eight inches deep, at least 100 feet from water or any place that "runoff" could carry contamination into a water source.

Drinking Water

As natural and thirst quenching as it may look, water sources in the forest, unless piped in specifically for human consumption, can carry contaminations. The most common is *Giardia lamblia*. This is an intestinal parasite with an incubation period of 6-15 days. Symptoms include: nausea, abdominal cramps, flatulence, lethargy, diarrhea and weight loss. The disease may persist for months if not treated. See your doctor promptly if you suspect you are ill. The most effect method of water treatment is to bring water to a vigorous boil. The use of chemical treatment or filtration systems may purify water, but are not considered as effective as boiling.

Cultural Artifacts

Items natural to the forest, both prehistoric and historic, add variety and interest to your wilderness adventure. They must not be disturbed and certainly not removed. It is a federal crime to remove items such as arrowheads and other artifacts.

What About Bears?

To avoid problems with bears, keep your campsite clean and counter-balance everything that has an odor, including soap, toothpaste, trash and freeze-dried food. Bear-proof canisters are available from most sporting goods stores, general stores and in some cases at your campsite. This is the most effective way to store your food. You can also use a method of hanging your food at least 12 feet high and at least 10 feet from the tree trunk. Choose a limb that is no more than 5 inches thick near the truck and about 2 inches at the end. This will prevent the bear from trying to climb the tree, go out on the limb and chow down! If a bear approaches your camp, yell, bang pots and pans, or wave clothing in the air. A raiding camp bear is only interested in your food, but all bears are potentially dangerous. If a bear does not leave, you should. Do not attempt to recover any food from a bear or approach them, especially a cub. If you have problems with bears or any other animals, report the incident to the rangers. Bears that become too dependent on improperly stored food can learn to be aggressive and usually have to be destroyed.

Altitude Sickness

You can over exert yourself on vacation and start to feel the following symptoms: fatigue, weakness, headache, loss of apetite, nausea, vomiting and shortness of breath. This is caused by a lack of oxygen. When you feel any of these, stop and rest. Breathe deeply, eat high energy foods, drink water, take aspirin and, most importantly, travel slowly to a lower elevation if the symptoms continue. If you are in good health and physical condition, you should be fine. Perhaps you should plan to stay a day or two doing less strenuous activities before hitting the trails to higher elevations, so your body can acclimate.

Mountaineering

Remember that not being prepared for the consequences of your decisions can lead to less than happy experiences and perhaps even your survival. Don't be in a rush. Watch the skies. Weather conditions can change rapidly. Be careful and mindful of others. Be safe!

Firearms

Hunting is permitted, in season, in the wilderness areas, the national forests, but *not* allowed in the national parks. Local Ranger Stations can give you details on the hunting regulations in the area. Target shooting is never allowed in any wilderness area. Do not discharge a firearm within 150' of any campsite, occupied area or trail or across any adjacent body of water.

Falling Rocks

When traveling in steep areas, watch for falling rocks. It is more usual to have rock slides during the warmest part of the day. Be aware when in steep terrain, move one at a time across hazardous spots. Stay out of gullies and away from cliff walls and previous slide areas. Don't camp in such an area. During the winter, you have the added chance of falling ice and snow from above.

Crossing Rivers and Streams

Swift running water can be very treacherous. The power of rushing waters is highest in spring through early summer. If you ford a water way, look for a natural bridge, like a series of rocks or down trees. The elements can be very slippery. Don't cross above rapids or a waterfall. Use common sense. Perhaps a long stick or walking cane will help you with your balance as you cross.

Insects

The forest is full of mosquitoes, ticks and deer flies. Any insect repellent with active ingredient DEET, will be useful in helping to keep some of them off you! Ticks can carry Lyme Disease and

Rocky Mountain Spotted Fever. Anyone with rashes, flu-like feelings, headaches or fevers within days of your vacation, or if you know you've been bitten by a tick, should see a doctor promptly. Quick and proper treatment can easily cure most such bites.

Poison Ivy or Oak

Many of the lower elevation areas you may visit will have patches of poison ivy and poison oak. These plants will leave an oily film on skin, clothing, pets, fishing gear, anything. If you suspect you have been in contact with these plants, you can use a product called Tecnu, it is available from most drug stores. It is effective even eight hours after contact.

Be Aware of the Weather

No matter where you are traveling, there's going to be weather! Watch for dry streams becoming torrents during storms. Get in a safe area when an impending thunderstorm is coming. Avoid open areas like meadows, ridges, mountain tops, shallow caves, isolated tree areas and water. When in the forest, staying away from the tallest trees is safer. If stuck in an open area, remove metal backpacks, fishing rods and get low to the ground. If possible, lie on an insulated poncho. If your vehicle is around, get in it.

Hypothermia

Anyone with a subnormal body temperature can end up with a mental or physical collapse or even death. This is caused by a combination of cold, wetness, wind and is worsened by exhaustion. This usually occurs in places where the air temperature is between 30-50 degrees F. It can happen any time of the year. Symptoms are vague, slow, slurred speech; memory lapses; uncontrollable fits of shivering; stumbling; drowsiness and exhaustion. Watch for early signs in your companions. Victims frequently don't know what is happening to them. Believe the signs, not the victim. Even mild hypothermia requires immediate treatment. To aid the victim, get them out of the wind, rain or snow. Strip off all clothes and put the person in a dry sleeping bag to help restore their body heat. Skin to skin contact with another unclothed person is the quickest way to restore body temperature and should be immediately in extreme cases. If the victim is conscious, give them warm foods and energy foods, like chocolate or energy bars.

Winter Travel

No matter what the season, you should always travel with a good flashlight, extra batteries, a shovel, road flares, blankets and water. In winter, you need to add snow chains to this list. If hiking in the winter, you'll find a solitude in the white wilderness that is an entirely different experience. But, you need to be aware of the dangers. Deep snow, ice faces, frozen streams or lakes can lead to situations you want to avoid. Choose reasonable goals for your trip. Carry extra food and fuel in case you have to create an emergency campsite. Three people are a minimum safe party size. Know the signs and symptoms of hypothermia. Carry a map and a compass. Know how to use them! Your pack should include a good knife, waterproof matches, a container to melt snow for drinking, a flashlight, large tarp, rain gear and wool clothes.

Emergency First Aid

No matter where you are, it is good to know basic first aid. If you are a frequent wilderness camper, you might want to take an Emergency Medical Tech course. The skills you learn could save you or someone you love.

Map Index